KINGDOMS IN CONFLICT

READING DANIEL TODAY

Andrew Reid

PRESS

Anglican Information Office
Sydney NSW 2000

PUBLISHED AUGUST 1993

BY THE ANGLICAN INFORMATION OFFICE
ST. ANDREW'S HOUSE, SYDNEY SQUARE 2000

© COPYRIGHT ANDREW REID 1993

NATIONAL LIBRARY OF AUSTRALIA
ISBN 0 949108 685

DESIGNED AND COVER ART BY HELEN SEMMLER

PRINTED IN AUSTRALIA BY
Southwood Press Pty. Ltd., Sydney

Contents

FOREWORD

Reading Daniel Today belongs to a series devoted on one hand to a simple, non-technical presentation of biblical books and, on the other, to careful scholarship.

Andrew Reid is well-equipped to write for this series, having pursued post-graduate studies in the history of the period in which Daniel was written.

Andrew's commentary on Daniel is the end product of some years of 'field testing' the material with various groups among whom he works as a university chaplain.

Andrew Reid is deeply conscious that the books of the Old Testament must be read through Christian eyes. So understood, and as presently written, Daniel will prove nourishing to Christians today. No part of the Old Testament is more significant to Jesus than Daniel. Here we meet the Kingdom of God, one like a Son of Man, the Saints of the Most High and the Abomination of Desolation.

I am confident that Reading Daniel Today will prove to be a significant and outstanding addition to this series.

Dr Paul Barnett
Series Editor
(Bishop of North Sydney)

For Chris Bellenger and the AFES

Reading Daniel Today I

1

Why Read Daniel ?

The book of Daniel is a book full of in-depth theological reflection on the nature of God and his rule of the world. It is loaded with insights into some of the most troubling issues of the faith and speaks to some of the most adult of all Christian problems, such as the problems of evil and persecution, of suffering, and of being Christians in an alien world. For us who face these issues with differing degrees of harshness, Daniel offers guidance and help.

Daniel also speaks to us of heroes of faith. Daniel, Shadrach, Meshach, Abednego and the saints of the Most High of the book of Daniel knew all about facing great difficulties. They lived in a world set against them and somehow managed to maintain their distinctiveness. These men stand out in the crowd. They held on to their faith in God despite the temptations and persecutions the world they lived in thrust upon them and despite the fact that triumph sometimes eluded them. These men model the life of faith and become a source of great encouragement and inspiration for those who struggle with the same problems after them.

Although the book of Daniel is worth reading for these reasons alone, it is also important because of the place it occupies in the thought of the Bible as a whole and in the thinking of Jesus in particular. When Jesus talked of the kingdom of God and called himself the Son of Man and waited for his vindication at the hand of God he seems to have done so with Daniel at the back of his mind. The book of Daniel helps us understand much about the person of Jesus and the nature of his work. It also helps us understand his teaching about the end of the world and the teaching of many of those who followed him, such as the writer of the book of Hebrews, the writer of 1 and 2 Peter and the writer of the book of Revelation.

FOR STUDY, DISCUSSION AND PRAYER

Before proceeding any further, get an easy to read version of the Bible and set aside an hour or so to read through Daniel in one sitting. As you read, note down any difficulties or questions you have about what you are reading.

If you get a chance, read it through a second time, ignoring any breaks and headings put in by the translators of your Bible. Where would you put the breaks in? What headings would you give to each of the sections of the book?

If you are studying this book with a group of people then discuss your findings together.

Spend time praying for God's enlightenment and help as you study and as you try to live out what you find in the book.

2

The Trouble
With Daniel

Any reader of Daniel who is reading at more than a superficial level encounters problems and questions, the answers to which are often detailed. In a commentary this size we can only indicate what these problems are and suggest a possible resolution to them. The reader who wishes further information and a more detailed analysis of the problems of Daniel might like to consult the commentaries by J.G. Baldwin (*Daniel*, Tyndale Old Testament Commentaries, Inter-Varsity Press, 1978) and J.E. Goldingay (*Daniel*, Word Bible Commentary, Word, 1989).

1. Who is Daniel?

Apart from the book of Daniel itself, the name 'Daniel' only appears a few times in the Bible (1 Chronicles 3:1; Ezra 8:2; Nehemiah 10:6; and Ezekiel 14:14, 20; 28:3). Of these references, only those in Ezekiel can possibly refer to a Daniel who remained at court in Babylon from the time of Nebuchadnezzar to the time of Cyrus.

When Ezekiel mentions Daniel he links him with Noah and Job and speaks about him as a person of outstanding and well-known righteousness. In Ezekiel 28 he is said to be a person of legendary wisdom. These characteristics of righteousness and wisdom are fitting summaries of the Daniel we find in the book of Daniel, especially since it appears that Daniel's wisdom was already well-known a number of years before Ezekiel's prophecy (cf Daniel 1-2).

It should be noted, however, that identifying the Daniel of Ezekiel with that of the book named after him is not without its problems. Firstly, the spelling of the Hebrew name is slightly different in the two books. Furthermore, the Daniel of Ezekiel appears to be a figure known not only to Israelites, but perhaps even to the King of Tyre (Ezekiel 28:3). It is these factors which have caused some to identify the Daniel of Ezekiel with an ancient figure called *Dan'el* who appears in Ancient Near Eastern mythology.

Apart from these biblical references, Josephus, the Jewish historian, tells us that Daniel was an Israelite of royal or noble descent (*Ant.* 10:188). As we shall see, this also is implied by the biblical accounts in Kings and Chronicles of the sort of people Nebuchadnezzar carried off into exile.

Some commentators, given the possibility that we may have no contemporary references to Daniel, go on to say that Daniel is a literary fiction. The position taken in this commentary is that the book of Daniel reflects a good historical tradition. Daniel did exist. He was taken as a youth from Jerusalem. He spent most of his life in the court at Babylon and he became renowned amongst the Jews for his righteousness and wisdom.

2. Who Wrote Daniel?

When it speaks about Daniel, the book uses both first person speech (for example, 'I, Daniel . . .' – 8:3) and third person narrative (for example, 'But Daniel resolved not to . . .' – 1:8). The use of third person narrative predominates until Daniel 7:3, after which there is a switch to first person speech.

Although the use of first person speech implies that Daniel himself wrote the material of these later chapters, we ought to be wary of too hastily assuming that it is Daniel's hand that wrote the words as they appear. Even within the book we have an example of this literary device being used. In chapter 4 Nebuchadnezzar also speaks in the first person. The prophets also often record the Word of God using first person speech, even though it is evident that there is no hint of his having dictated that word to them. In the New Testament Luke records the speeches of Paul in the first person, even though it is evident that what we have are summaries of those speeches.

Some commentators on the book of Daniel (especially those who date the writing of the book in the second century BC) have noted that there are a significant number of books written in a similar style to Daniel. These are apocalyptic writings which typically are ascribed to great individuals of antiquity such as Enoch, Moses, Ezra and Baruch. Since Daniel is so similar in style to these other works, it is assumed that it too was written by someone other than the implied author. Like these other works it is regarded as a product of the Hellenistic age.

It can be seen, therefore, that the question of *who* wrote Daniel, is inextricably linked with the question of *when* it was written.

3. When was Daniel Written?

The question of dating is a complicated one involving technical information and arguments about the contents of the book: its literary style, the accuracy of its historical detail, and the dating of various linguistic features contained within it. These arguments have resulted in two broad positions about date.

The first group of scholars say that the contents of the visions in particular (that is, chapters 7-12) imply a situation where power lies in the hands of hostile powers and there is a group of people which support these powers and a group that opposes them. This suits the situation in Palestine under Hellenistic rule during the second century BC. In support of this position they put forward the following evidence:

- The text of the whole book contains historical errors or inconsistencies which may imply some distance from the actual events.

- The second half of the book seems to betray a remarkably good knowledge of events in the second century, so much so that it looks particularly like history written after the event.

- The use of Persian and Greek loan words and the way that Hebrew and Aramaic are used within the book indicate a date after the conquest of Palestine by Alexander the Great.

A second group of scholars notes that the content of the stories implies a very different situation to that experienced in second century BC Palestine. They assume a situation where the Jews are out of their own land and where their faith, although under threat, is able to survive and even succeed. Furthermore, it is a situation where Jews may hold positions of authority under foreign rule. As well as countering most of the arguments put forward by the former group, these scholars maintain that there are elements of the book that cannot be explained within the framework of a second century BC date.

Both groups seem to increasingly agree in the opinion that the literary evidence is all in favour of the book being considered a unity. This being the case we are therefore faced with a choice.

We can say that the book was written by a group of pious second century believers who first, put together older (oral or maybe even written) stories about God's dealings with faithful individuals in the past and his revelations to them about the shape of the future. They second, edited, added to, and built on, these revelations on the basis of their understanding of what God was doing in their own situation.

Alternatively we can say that the book was written in the sixth century BC by Daniel or someone who knew much about him. These writings not only directly addressed issues that Jews faced in exile, but also contained predictions of what was to happen to the people of God over the next four centuries in Palestine. They gave a special focus on Jerusalem in the second century.

The position taken in this commentary is that the sixth century historical person of Daniel is the source for both the stories and the visions. Both therefore reflect in language and emphasis the situation in exile during the sixth century. They also show dramatic insight into the course of Jewish history in Palestine over the next four centuries. It is unknown when they assumed the final form as we have it now. However, a second century date cannot be decisively ruled out, especially given the applicability of Daniel's vision to the situation Jews in Palestine faced in the second century BC and the inevitable encouragement such a word from God would have given them.

3

The Shape
of Daniel

The book of Daniel is intricate in structure and the deeper we delve into it, the more we become aware of its intricacies. A few examples will suffice. At a first reading we are struck by the neat division of the book into two sections: stories (chapters 1-7) and visions (chapters 8-12). On a second reading, other indications of structure come to the fore such as the use of the third person in chapters 1:1-7.3 and the use of the first person in chapters 8-12.

Subsequent readings of the English text of Daniel would indicate a striking similarity in themes between various chapters. For example: Chapters 1 and 9 deal with questions posed by the exile. Chapters 2 and 7, one a dream by Nebuchadnezzar and the other a dream by Daniel, both concern the rise and fall of four kingdoms. Chapters 3 and 6 are striking in their similarity of plot: Jews trapped by others, sentenced to death and finally vindicated. Chapters 4 and 5 concern God's dealings with human rulers; one who recognises God's authority and the other who does not.

If we could read the original languages used in the book we would notice a further division: Daniel 1-2:4a and chapters 8-12 are written in Hebrew, while chapters 2:4b-7:28 are written in Aramaic.

The analysis of the book given below tries to capture some of these features. As we deal with the individual chapters some of the structural connections of the book and the way they serve the writer's overall purpose will be further explained.

H		1	A The Exile and God's People
	S	2	B Dreaming of the End of Human Kingdoms
A	**T**		
R	**O**	3	C Living in Two Kingdoms
A	**R**	4	D The War of Kings
M	**I**		
A	**E**	5	D' The War of Kings
I	**S**	6	C' Living in Two Kingdoms
C		7	B' Dreaming of the End of Human Kingdoms
	V		
	I	8	A' The Exile and God's Purpose
	S		
H	**I**		
E	**O**		
B	**N**	9	More Questions and Answers Concerning the End
R	**S**		
E			
W		10-12	A Heavenly Messenger and a Final Revelation

4

How to Read
this Book

Like the rest of the books in this series, this book is a simple, non-technical commentary directed towards ordinary readers. As with the other books, there are brief chapters with questions at the end of each chapter that are aimed at helping personal reflection, family or group discussion.

As discussed, although written in the sixth century BC, historically the book of Daniel covers the period from the first deportation to Babylon right through to the time of Antiochus IV in the second century BC. Within this period there are two focuses of the book: the days in which Daniel and his friends were exiled in Babylon and the reign of Antiochus.

In the next chapter of this commentary, there is an introduction to the history which lies behind the first section of the book and the situation in which Daniel finds himself in Babylon. The details of the time of Antiochus IV will be taken up in the commentary proper, although you may find it helpful to have a quick read through the apocryphal books of 1 and 2 Maccabees, especially 1 Maccabees 1 and 2 Maccabees 4-9 before reading the chapters of this commentary which address Daniel 7-12. (The Jerusalem Bible contains the books of Maccabees).

The theme of the kingdom of God emerges constantly throughout the book of Daniel and to some extent ties it together. For this reason I have supplied some extra chapters which reflect on this theme and attempt to draw out some of its practical implications.

Finally, I have closed the commentary with some reflections of the implications of the book of Daniel and its central themes for the person and ministry of Jesus and for us as we attempt to live as Christians in the twentieth century.

If you still have not read Daniel on your own, then put this book down and get out Daniel and begin. It is a tremendous read!

5

The World of Daniel

1. A Superpower Strikes

(a) 'In the Third Year'

The first verse of Daniel tells us that *in the third year of the reign of Jehoiakim king of Judah, Nebuchadnezzar king of Babylon came to Jerusalem and besieged it.* This verse does a number of things for the reader:

- It introduces us to the period from which the book of Daniel emerges: the destruction of Jerusalem by the Babylonian empire and the subsequent exile of its inhabitants.

- It also introduces us to one of the principal characters of the book of Daniel, King Nebuchadnezzar of Babylon.

- It raises the sorts of questions which the book of Daniel, and especially the first chapter, seeks to raise and answer.

This first verse is also difficult because of the apparent discrepancy between it and other dates suggested in the Bible (for example, Jeremiah 46:2 which talks about the fourth year of Jehoiakim) and those suggested in Babylonian sources. However this text is not as difficult historically as some have maintained and it is possible to reconstruct the events of the exile in such a way as to take into account the data both from

the Bible and Babylonian sources. The following outline of
the history behind Daniel 1 provides such a reconstruction
as well as introducing us to Nebuchadnezzar and giving us a
feel for the way the exiles would have been thinking and
feeling about God, Babylon, and the king under whom they
were to live in exile.

(b) The Events of 605 BC [Map 1]

The period just before the exile was a time of great change.
For some time the dominant power in the world of the fertile
crescent had been Assyria, but now this great nation had
weakened and Babylon was on the rise, threatening not only
Assyria, but the other great player in this world, Egypt. As a
result, the Egyptians decided to march North to support
Assyria against Babylon.

At this time Nebuchadnezzar, the crown prince of Babylon,
took control of the Babylonian army. In keeping with his
growing reputation as a strategist and cunning general, he
pushed on and launched a surprise attack on the Egyptians
at Carchemish on the upper Euphrates river. The Egyptians
were crushed and the remnants of their army pursued all the
way back along the Mediterranean coast to Egypt (cf Jeremiah
46:13-24).

Such events had been foreseen by Jeremiah and other
prophets in Judah and Jerusalem. The movements of the
surrounding great powers deeply affected this tiny nation
encircled by the three of them and allied with one of them,
Egypt. So with Babylon on the move and Egypt in flight
things on the outside looked grim. Before long
Nebuchadnezzar would assert his power on this tiny but
strategic nation.

The words of Habakkuk the prophet had circulated
around the city of Jerusalem and ran through the minds of
many Jews as they gravely faced prospects of the future.

Look at the nations and watch – and be utterly amazed. For I am going to do something in your days that you would not believe, even if you were told. I am raising up the Babylonians, that ruthless and impetuous people, who sweep across the whole earth to seize dwelling places not their own. They are a feared and dreaded people, they are a law to themselves and promote their own honour. Their horses are swifter than leopards, fiercer than wolves at dusk. Their cavalry gallops headlong; their horsemen come from afar. They fly like a vulture swooping to devour; they all come bent on violence. Their hordes advance like a desert wind and gather prisoners like sand. They deride kings and scoff at rulers. They laugh at fortified cities; they build earthen ramps and capture them. Then they sweep past like the wind and go on – guilty men, whose own strength is their god.

...You have made men like fish in the sea, like sea creatures that have no ruler. The wicked foe pulls all of them up with hooks, he catches them in his net, he gathers them up in his dragnet; and so he rejoices and is glad. Therefore he sacrifices to his net and burns incense to his dragnet, for by his net he lives in luxury and enjoys the choicest food. Is he to keep on emptying his net, destroying the nations without mercy? (Habakkuk 1:5-11,14-17; cf Jeremiah 5-6)

As it happened there was a mild reprieve for Judah and all the vassal states of Egypt. In hot pursuit of the Egyptians, Nebuchadnezzar received word that his father had died in Babylon and was forced to make a hurried dash across the desert to secure the throne. The next year, however he returned and did subdue all the territory that had been Egypt's, including Judah (2 Kings 24:1-7, especially verses 1 and 7). As Nebuchadnezzar left, the whole city wept for the small band that was carted off as hostages. It appears that among these hostages were Daniel, Hananiah, Mishael, and Azariah (Daniel 1:1-7).

Map 1: *The Events of 605 BC*

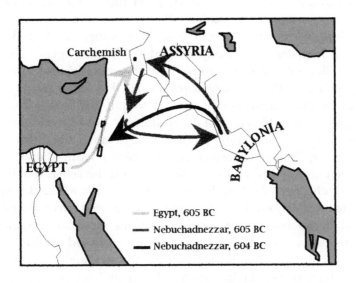

(c) Waiting for the End [Map 2]

The next few years were tumultuous for Jerusalem. Babylon continued to grow in strength. Each year the inevitable seemed closer and yet the ruling parties in Jerusalem and the people they led seemed to deny it. They looked back to the temple, to the ark of the covenant, and to the promises given to David, assuring themselves that everything would be all right. Somehow they believed that despite their idolatry and flagrant disobedience God would preserve the nation because they had captured and confined God in a temple in their capital city (Jeremiah 7).

On the other hand, the astute and godly listened intently to prophets such as Jeremiah. They lifted their hands in prayer and begged Yahweh yet again to act in mercy towards his straying people. But God had had enough. His ears were closed on the issue and before long his anger would be poured out on Judah. It was an anger that would burn and not be quenched (Jeremiah 7:20).

God's judgment was not long in coming. In 601 BC Nebuchadnezzar led another expedition against Egypt. This time Pharaoh Neco was prepared and Nebuchadnezzar and Egypt both suffered heavy losses. Boosted by Egypt's success and by Nebuchadnezzar's retreat to put his forces back together again, the kings of many subject states withheld their annual tribute, including Jehoiakim of Judah. Duly refitted, however, Nebuchadnezzar set out again from Babylon. Systematically and ruthlessly he put down the rebels one by one. Jehoiakim died on the eve of the siege and was replaced by his son, Jehoiachin (= Jeconiah). Jehoiachin surrendered and Nebuchadnezzar carried out his first large scale deportation from Judah. Those deported included Jehoiachin and his family, leading statesmen and courtiers, members of the higher ranks of Judean society and the prophet Ezekiel – about 10,000 people in all. As prophesied (2 Kings 20:17), the temple was seized and royal treasures that were left were taken and placed in the temples of the gods of Babylon (2 Kings 24:8-17 cf Daniel 1:1-2). Finally, Nebuchadnezzar appointed a vice-regent, Mattaniah (renamed Zedekiah), to rule over Judah.

Map 2: *Waiting for the End*

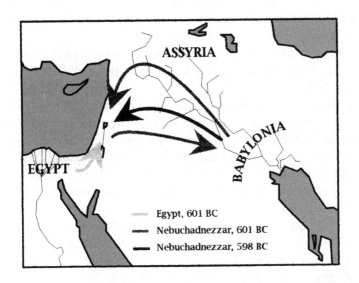

(d) Final Destruction

Again endless discussion followed. Jeremiah spoke out, warning that continued allegiance to Nebuchadnezzar was the only way to remain secure. Again he and those similarly minded were not heeded. When they spoke in opposition they were persecuted and silenced. Judah rebelled, and again Babylon marched on Jerusalem and besieged it.

This time Nebuchadnezzar lived up to all the rumours about him. He watched and waited as the siege went on and then stormed the city. He arranged for the temple, palace buildings and great houses to be torched and levelled. He demolished the city wall and took the rest of the temple vessels and any remaining precious metals. He executed principal citizens and deported the upper and middle classes to Babylon. He then tracked down the fleeing Zedekiah and killed his sons in front of him before gouging out his eyes and binding him in shackles, to be dragged off to a dungeon in Babylon (2 Kings 24:18-25:21).

What had been promised time and time again since the days of Moses (for example, Deuteronomy 28) had been fulfilled. Israel had continued to sin and the Lord had brought a nation against them from far away, from the ends of the earth, whose language they did not understand. This fierce-looking nation had swooped on them like an eagle, showing no respect for the old or pity for the young. As God had promised, so he had delivered them into the hand of Nebuchadnezzar, king of Babylon (Deuteronomy 28:49-50; cf Daniel 1:1-2).

The captives who marched across the desert must have had much to think about. The last days of Jerusalem would have been indelibly inscribed on their minds: the siege, the horrors of famine, the cannibalism as the siege began to hit the city hard (cf 2 Kings 15:16; Lamentations 4:10). There would have been relatives killed, children slaughtered, sisters raped, and pregnant wives disembowelled (Jeremiah 15:6-9 cf 2 Kings 8:12; Isaiah 13:16,18; Hosea 13:16).

They would also have remembered the once proud walls and temple and the pile of rubble they had become and the taunts of the people of their brother nation, the Edomites. They laughed at them, looted their goods, and rounded up those who fled and handed them over to the Babylonians. Many of them yearned for vengeance and vindication. They longed for the day when Edom would be judged and Babylon repaid (Psalm 137; Obadiah).

But most of all, many of them would have wondered about their future and the uncertain existence that lay before them. In this context they undoubtedly wondered about their God and grappled with the large questions of faith. They were real questions that needed answers:

Was Yahweh finished?

Did the defeat of Israel amount to a defeat of Yahweh?

As Babylon battled Israel on the battlefield and won, had Marduk the god of Babylon battled Yahweh the God of Israel and won?

Was Yahweh dead on the battlefield, a defeated God?

If Israel was a 'has-been' in the world of the new superpowers, was Yahweh a 'has-been' in the new world of supergods?

As if to confirm such fears, Nebuchadnezzar proudly put the vessels of Yahweh's temple on display in the temple of Marduk. They would stand forever as a symbol of the power of his own gods and the powerlessness, death, and defeat of Yahweh (Daniel 1:2).

The opening verses of Daniel 1 are therefore markedly despondent. They raise huge questions regarding the nature of God and of his future purposes, both in the world in general and among his people in particular. These questions set the context for Daniel 1.

Reading Daniel Today II

6

Knocked Down But Not Knocked Out 1:1-21

1. The Agenda Is Set

(a) Difficult Questions

The first few verses not only set the background for Daniel, they also let us into the mind of the author as he gives us some subtle hints as to where he is heading and how he is going to answer the sorts of questions raised by the exile. The first hint is in the first half of verse 2 where we read that *the Lord delivered Jehoiakim, king of Judah, into his hand.*

Already we are being told that God is not absent. Rather than being defeated or lazy or forgetful, he has been active and is the one responsible for the situation in which Israel finds itself.

The second hint is given when we are told that God also delivered *some of the articles from the temple of God* into Nebuchadnezzar's hand and that these *he carried off to the temple of his god in Babylonia and put in the treasure house of his god.*

These words state the dilemma of the chapter and of the first six chapters. Because his people were in Babylon and the symbols of his previous glory were in pagan temples, it appeared that God was defeated. How would God deal with the situation? What would he do? Would he take on the gods of Nebuchadnezzar and the Babylonians and did he stand a chance against the supergods of these superpowers?

The third hint is in the latter half of verse two. The NIV translation only records it in the reading in the margin. Taking this reading from the margin and including it in the text would give us the following translation: *And the Lord delivered Jehoiakim, king of Judah, into his hand, along with some of the articles from the temple of God. These he carried off to the temple of his god in the land of Shinar and put them in the treasure house of his god.*

'The land of Shinar' is a strange and ancient way of speaking, used only a few times in the Old Testament (Genesis 10:10; 11:2; 14:1,9; Isaiah 11:11; Zechariah 5:11, of which the key one is Genesis 11:2). It is the place where people built the tower of Babel (Genesis 11). This tower represented humanity at its strongest setting itself against God; humans asserting themselves against God and his kingship.

By using this phrase the writer reminded us of the protagonists in this chapter – a human king and the king of heaven – and again he has us asking: What will God do? Will he repeat Babel? Can he win again?

These verses therefore set an agenda: the greatest of human kingdoms pitted against the seemingly defeated kingdom of God, the gods of the nations pitted against the God of the puny, defeated nation of Israel. Into this conflict marched Daniel and his friends.

2. A Program of Assimilation

(a) Stage 1:   1:3-4a

Nebuchadnezzar's first step in the game plan was a good one. It involved a program of assimilation of the Israelites. He set stage one into motion. The king ordered *Ashpenaz, chief of his court officials, to bring in some of the Israelites from the royal family and the nobility.* They were to be good looking, physically perfect, high in intelligence and teachable: *young men without any physical defect, handsome, showing aptitude for every kind of learning, well informed, quick to understand, and qualified to serve in the king's palace.* It was a shrewd move by Nebuchadnezzar.

(b) Stage 2:   1:4b

Stage two involved throwing these young men into the world of the Chaldeans for three years training (the period normally required for a competent scribe). Ashpenaz was to *teach them in the language and literature of the Babylonians.* This world of the Babylonians or Chaldeans was one of renown, a world of priests, expert magicians, astrology, philosophy and the best literature of the ancient world. The literature covered would include omens, incantations, prayers, hymns, myths, legends and scientific formulas for skills such as glass making, mathematics and astrology. Daniel and his friends were to study this literature and become masters of it.

(c) Stage 3:   1:5

Yet there was more than an education in store for the young Israelites. They were to enter even greater privileges, reserved for a chosen few. They were given a special honour in being *assigned a daily amount of food and wine from the king's table.* The most expensive menu in the known world is to be their diet. Stage three was implemented.

The program was to take place over *three years*, after which they would *enter the king's service.*

What was happening to Daniel and his friends was not unique. Hebrew heroes of the Old Testament were often found at the court of foreign kings. Joseph had been there in Genesis 41-48 and Nehemiah would serve in a pagan court later, as would Ezra. Jews often had political and social orders imposed on them. As time went on it would become increasingly common, and although they would have preferred it otherwise they knew they could handle it because of their view of the world. They believed that the world was God's world, a good creation of the God of Israel (Genesis 1). As God's world it was a place to be involved in rather than avoided. For a Jew who believed in a Creator God training in a pagan king's palace was all right. There was nothing wrong with being there.

(d) Stage 4: 1:6-7

Stage four was equally cunning. To deal with people for whom names were an important part of their identity, Nebuchadnezzar decided to do some renaming. *The chief official* gave them *new names: to Daniel, the name Belteshazzar; to Hananiah, Shadrach; to Mishael, Meshach; and to Azariah, Abednego.* In so doing, Nebuchadnezzar struck a crucial blow. He took names composed of the names of the Hebrew God (EL or YAHWEH) and he turned them into names that either included the names of Babylonian gods or were somewhat meaningless. For example, Daniel (= 'God is my Judge') became Belteshazzar, which probably meant 'O lady (Ishtar) protect the king' or 'May (Marduk) protect his life'. Given what had gone on already this represented a final tragedy for

Daniel and his friends. Israelite distinctiveness was all but lost.

In the first two verses of the chapter the vessels of the God of Israel are found in the house of the gods of the nations. In the next four verses the sons of Israel are found under the names of the gods of the nations. So we ask: 'Where is the God of Israel? Can He survive?'. In the second four verses we find the people of God under a program of assimilation and we ask: 'Where are the people of God, can they survive?' 'Will assimilation succeed?' In three years' time these young men were to stand before the king. The test for them would be to remain faithful, to retain their Jewish identity and not to become puppets of this pagan tyrant, assimilated into his ways.

3. There Is No Such Thing As A Free Lunch

Daniel and his friends had seen Nebuchadnezzar in action themselves. They were undoubtedly scared of Nebuchadnezzar and afraid of what would happen if they did not meet his expectations.

But as a Jew from the nobility, Daniel had probably received training in the stories of the great ones of Israel: Abraham, Isaac, Jacob, Joseph, Moses and David. From these stories he would have been aware that there was nothing wrong with being in a pagan court and learning pagan things, but that there were dangers to avoid and traps to sidestep. He could not let himself be trapped as Joseph had been by Potiphar's wife. He must not get caught as Solomon had in his dealings with foreigners such that they took away his distinctiveness as God's person. He must not act out of his own best interests, merely to preserve his life. This the kings had done time after time and so brought Israel back into slavery away from the promised land.

(a) Daniel's Resolution

With these things in mind at some point *Daniel resolved* that he would hang on to his belief in God. He was going to preserve his faith and maintain his integrity. He decided to say 'no'.

At the appropriate point he therefore faced the chief eunuch and let him know that he would not accept the kings' rich food and drink and asked for *permission not to defile himself in this way*. He had accepted deportation, a re-education and a name change, but he would not bend on this third issue.

It was a radical thing to do. In doing so he chose to turn down the graciousness of his benefactor and so to oppose the great Nebuchadnezzar, the king of kings, the conqueror of the known world and the destroyer of Israel.

It was also a strange thing to do. If we were choosing a place to say 'no' it probably would not be here; after all, what could be wrong with food and drink?

(b) What Could Be Wrong With Food And Drink?

The first thing that could be wrong is that the food had been offered to idols and Daniel turned it down for this reason. This is unlikely. More likely is that we are taking a New Testament problem with which we are familiar (for example, 1 Corinthians 8-10) and reading it into an Old Testament context. Beside this, it does not explain what was wrong with the wine and neither does it deal with the fact that, from what we know the Babylonians offered every kind of food to their gods, including vegetables.

The second solution is to conclude that Daniel said 'no' because the meat was from unclean animals. Presuming that Daniel had had a good upbringing back in Jerusalem, he would have known that it was permissible for a Jew to eat meat from certain animals only and that all other meat was out of the question (for example, Leviticus 11; Deuteronomy 14:1-20). Again, this does not explain why he rejected the wine as well. The only people we know of who do not drink wine in the Old Testament are Nazarites (Numbers 6:21) and Rechabites (Jeremiah 35) and we have no indication that Daniel had these sympathies.

So what is the problem here? Why does Daniel say 'no' at this point? The solution can be found by going elsewhere in the book of Daniel. The other place where the words used in this passage to describe the food given to the young Israelites are used is in chapter 11, verse 26 (see the RSV that uses 'rich food' in translating both 1:5 and 11:26). This verse makes clear that those who shared the king's table also entered a covenant relationship with him. By eating his food they committed themselves to a friendship and so accepted that they had an obligation to be loyal to him. In 11:26 they broke that obligation by devising plots against the king (cf Psalm 41:9 and John 13:18). We have a similar but weaker sense in our own world. If one businessman asks another out to lunch and offers to pay there is often a sense of obligation such that when the businessman comes round a week later and asks for a favour it is hard to turn him down. There is no such thing as a free lunch!

(c) The Man Who Wants To Be Free

Daniel realised this. He refused the meals and wine because he knew that to accept would have symbolised his dependence upon the king and his commitment to him. The food and drink would defile Daniel in the sense that it challenged his freedom to be God's person.

In other words Daniel was saying that he wanted to be free. He wanted to say a clear 'no' to assimilation and to being a lackey of the king. By eating vegetables he showed that he and his friends were a distinct and special group, a force with which to be reckoned. They were God's people first, no matter the cost.

It is interesting to contrast Daniel's attitude with that of his king in 2 Kings 25:27-30. In one last crushing comment on Israelite kingship the writer showed Jehoiachin eating regularly at the king's table – the king's lackey for all the days of his life – a man who had no identity any more. He was a conquered man of a conquered nation. Unlike Daniel, he was no force to be feared or with which to be reckoned.

4. God Acts Again

Daniel had pronounced his ultimatum. Understandably the chief of eunuchs worried about his own head and was reluctant to support the proposal. He said to Daniel, *'I am afraid of my lord the king, who has assigned your food and drink. Why should he see you looking worse than the other young men your age? The king would then have my head because of you.'*

We can be sure that he was not the only one who was afraid. Daniel must have been petrified. All the writers of Scripture would have commended him for acting rightly but none of them would have promised him that he would be safe after his action. He acted without guarantees and stepped into a darkness from which he might never have emerged.

As readers of the story we do not have to face the darkness Daniel must have faced as he waited on the king's reaction. Somehow we know that the God of Israel will not leave Daniel. The words of verse 1 taught us that it was his will that the Israelites were here and the presence of such words was like a time bomb set to explode when the right moment came. It exploded in verse 9: We are told that God *caused the official to show favour and sympathy to Daniel*. Presumably it was this favour and sympathy that allowed Daniel to approach a lesser court official and obtain his cooperation in verses 11-14. He *agreed* to Daniel's suggestion that he *test your servants for ten days.* They were given *nothing but vegetables to eat and water to drink* before they were compared to *the young men who* had eaten *the royal food.*

Daniel had stepped out, prepared to take the risk that God would undergird his efforts and it happened. He and his friends surpassed their fellow students in health and appearance, looking *healthier and better nourished than any of the young men who ate the royal food,* with the result that *the guard took away their choice food and the wine they were to drink and gave them vegetables instead.*

5. God Acts A Third Time

Verse 17 provides us with the third reference to God's activity in the chapter. God acted to give *these four young men . . . knowledge and understanding of all kinds of literature and learning. And Daniel could understand visions and dreams of all kinds.* Through God's mercy and action the young men won out over assimilation.

It is very important to understand the real point of this chapter – God's reputation had been on the line. These young men represented God and it was he who gave them success. He gave them physical health and intellectual rigour. He acted again, for the third time in the chapter, to preserve his people. The hero may have been Daniel, but the power to do it was God's.

6. Victory Where It Counts

As we found subtle hints and questions in the first few verses of the chapter, so there is more than first meets the eye in the final verses of the chapter.

(a) Babylonians Vanquished

First we are informed of the vanquishing of the Babylonians or Chaldeans, for, *at the end of the time set by the king to bring them in, the chief official presented them to Nebuchadnezzar. The king talked with them, and he found none to equal Daniel, Hananiah, Mishael and Azariah; so they entered the king's service. In every matter of wisdom and understanding about which the king questioned them, he found them ten times better than all the magicians and enchanters in his whole kingdom.*

The point is not so much that Daniel and his friends were intellectually superior but that the source of their intellectual superiority and practical wisdom was God. The writer is stressing that the gods of the Babylonians who supplied wisdom to the Babylonians were no match for the God of Israel who gave *knowledge and all kinds of literature and learning* to his people.

The situation has changed from what it was in the first few verses of the chapter where outward victory had clearly gone to the gods of the Babylonians. However, as readers of the Bible we know that outward victory is not where reality is found and that outward defeat is not always a sign of being out of the battle altogether (cf 2 Corinthians 4.7-18). Nebuchadnezzar could not have defeated Jerusalem unless God had given it to him; it was God who enabled Daniel's insistence that he would not compromise to succeed; and it was God who gave Daniel and his friends such learning. So the questions that were there in the earlier verses have been answered – God did survive!

(b) Babel Repeated

What happened to the conflict between a human kingdom and the kingdom of God? Verse 21 addresses that issue as it tells us of the events of 539 BC. In that year the prophecies of Deuteronomy 30:3-5, Jeremiah 25:12 and Isaiah 45 were fulfilled. *King Cyrus* the Persian conquered the Babylonian kingdom and the great and awesome Babylon went the way of all human kingdoms while Daniel survived. Daniel, the representative of God and his kingdom in a pagan world had not only outmanoeuvred the representatives of the pagan gods, he had outlasted and outfoxed the kingdom of Babylon. He lived to see its fall and so he and his God survived the seemingly unconquerable.

As we can see, God repeated what he had done at Babel in Genesis 11. This time there was no shattering of the languages of people or dispersion of the nations throughout the world. In Daniel 1 all we had was the lonely figure of Daniel, trusting God and therefore conquering human kingdoms by the kingdom of God.

7. Daring To Be A Daniel

The Daniel we saw in this chapter was someone that we often wish we could be and he had something that we often wish we had. Daniel was not afraid of death, of Nebuchadnezzar, or of the pagan environment in which he lived and of which he had became an expert. Daniel was secure in his trust in God and was therefore unlike many in his time who thought the only way forward in exile was to withdraw into a ghetto and struggle to preserve a ghetto-like faith, separated from any contact with polluting Babylonian life.

Nor was Daniel like those who gave in to Babylon, and said that history had suggested that the Babylonians were the way ahead. They had the knowledge, learning and culture. They were wealthy and powerful. Perhaps old religions and old ways should be left behind.

Daniel's security reflected neither of these positions. He seemed to know the benefits of this world and its dangers.

He suspected the world and knew how far to accompany it. Like others in the Bible Daniel was aware that the presuppositions and conclusions of this world need to be recognised and avoided. However, Daniel was not in retreat. He was an agent for God in bringing others to know God. He was on the offensive, not withdrawing from the society in which he lived but participating in it. He confronted it and threw himself into it, in the hope that God would work through him to transform and recreate. As such he is a model for us in our attitude to the world in which we live.

The message of this chapter is that this world is God's world. As his world it is going to present us with many challenges to which we are going to have to say 'yes'. At the same time it also warns us that there are going to be some times when we must say 'no'. At these times we must not whisper but shout. We must make sure that we are heard. We must not let anything destroy even the smallest bit of our identity as God's person. Daniel reminds us as Christians in the twentieth century that because we have been bought by the blood of a lamb unblemished we must not allow ourselves to be bought by another at any price. We must not give way. Rather, we must live for Christ.

Daniel 1 encourages us in that it tells us that all this is possible. It is possible to operate as a person controlled by the kingdom of God in a world dominated by petty human kingdoms. Such a possibility depends on the grace of God and our trust in him.

FOR STUDY, DISCUSSION AND PRAYER

1. In what ways do Christians . . .
   (a) withdraw from the world?
   (b) go along with the world?

2. What does Daniel 1 tell us about the world and our attitude to it?

3. Share with others in the group the ways in which you are often tempted to say 'yes' to the world you live in when you really should say 'no'.

4. What do we learn from Daniel about determining what things matter and what do not?

5. What do we learn from Daniel 1 about God's control of his world?

7

The War of Kings
2:1-49

1. Nebuchadnezzar the Great (2:1)

By *the second year of his reign* the guarantees of the gods were
seen in action as Nebuchadnezzar continued on his military
campaigns in the West. Vast tributes were collected and even
more captives brought to Babylonia. He dispensed justice
and opposed hostile kings who attempted to rob his regions
of riches. He collected the renowned wood of Lebanon for
the temples of his gods and he reunited scattered fugitive
people and made the whole land happy. He was
Nebuchadnezzar the just, ruler of all lands from the edge of
Egypt to Lydia and the great river Euphrates. He had been
appointed by the gods and was fulfilling his promises to them
as they fulfilled theirs to him.

He had begun to make Babylon the wonder of the known
world. Under his efforts it was to become a major
international and local administrative centre, a city of great
learning, wisdom and beauty.

He was Nebuchadnezzar the great. He was the devout
worshipper of the gods Marduk and Nabu. He had
conquered the known world. He was a man of justice, a
philanthropist, benefactor, architect and builder. None had
ever matched him or challenged him. He was secure,

popular, respected and feared. Nothing had threatened him
and none had dared to depose him. But then, *in the second
year of his reign, Nebuchadnezzar had dreams; his mind was
troubled and he could not sleep.*

2. A King's Peace Disturbed (2:2-13)

In Nebuchadnezzar's world dreams were respected as
communication from the world of the gods.
Nebuchadnezzar would have believed that as he dreamt the
gods were talking to him. He would have wanted to find out
what they were saying, but he also probably feared what he
might find out.

It was for such an occasion that he had fostered the huge
range of astrologers, wise men and scientists. For many years
they had been nurtured and paid well so that they might come
to the rescue of their master. These men knew him well and
reaped immense benefits from his sponsorship of their
science. As men who had eaten the rich food from his table
and had drunk the same choice wines he had drunk, they had
a debt to pay and an obligation to fulfil. *So the king summoned
the magicians, enchanters, sorcerers and astrologers to tell him what
he had dreamed.*

*When they came in and stood before the king, he said to them, 'I
have had a dream that troubles me and I want to know what it
means.'*

Babylonians, like the Egyptians had dream manuals for
such occasions. These manuals usually gave long lists of
dreams and their meanings. Once in possession of the
content of the dream, interpretation could be resolved by
such professional interpreters as were in Nebuchadnezzar's
pay. And so *the astrologers answered the king in Aramaic, 'O
king, live forever! Tell your servants the dream, and we will
interpret it.'*

The king's wise men proved useless. For all their science and wisdom they could not even tell him the dream, let alone interpret it for him. However, sleepless nights and worrying days had increased the level of stress that he experienced and with it his frustration, desperation and anger and so he summoned his magicians, astrologers, philosophers and dream interpreters again. In vivid language he cursed and blessed them, threatening torture and reprisal as well as promising wealth and reward.

'This is what I have firmly decided: If you do not tell me what my dream was and interpret it, I will have you cut into pieces and your houses turned into piles of rubble. But if you tell me the dream and explain it, you will receive from me gifts and rewards and great honour. So tell me the dream and interpret it for me!'

It lacked effect. No flourishing of financial rewards or brandishing of dreaded punishments achieved the impossible. They were unable to interpret the dream without knowing its content. Again they pleaded, *'Let the king tell his servants the dream, and we will interpret it.'*

Nebuchadnezzar knew what they said was true. If they knew the dream they could turn to their books and decipher a meaning from them. For this reason perhaps he was glad that he could not remember the dream. With wealth or death hanging over their heads, these men had a huge incentive to provide an interpretation and who was he to know whether it would be accurate. However, if there were someone who could present the dream itself, then they could be trusted to give a faithful explanation.

On the other hand, it is of course possible that Nebuchadnezzar did know the dream but hid it from his astrologers so he could be assured of a true interpretation.

The king's frustration, anxiety and feelings of helplessness rose to fever pitch and he became morose, unpredictable and unreasonable. In a fit of anger he made a decision. The free-loaders in his court must be made to pay their way. They had lived off him for too long. He was king; he needed a revealer; and they had not met his expectations He would replace them: *'I am certain that you are trying to gain time, because you realise that this is what I have firmly decided. If you do not tell me the dream, there is just one penalty for you. You have conspired to tell me misleading and wicked things, hoping the situation will change. So then, tell me the dream, and I will know that you can interpret it for me.'*

The truth came, the facts which Nebuchadnezzar knew and feared. The astrologers answered the king, and told him, *'There is not a man on earth who can do what the king asks! No king, however great and mighty, has ever asked such a thing of any magician or enchanter or astrologer. What the king asks is too difficult. No one can reveal it to the king except the gods, and they do not live among men.'*

Not even the truth could save the men of learning. He was Nebuchadnezzar who could not be defied and so his decree went out *ordering the execution of all the wise men of Babylon.* All the wise men of Babylonia were to be gathered and *put to death.* The guards left and systematically worked through their death list, including the young Israelites, *Daniel and his friends.*

3. A Man Who Interpreted Dreams (2:14-35)

(a) Taking A Risk (2:14-20)

By this stage in his career Daniel knew the king and his character and therefore knew that the decree was impulsive and harsh. He determined to see what could be done about it. He took a risk and so, *when Arioch, the commander of the king's guard, had gone out to put to death the wise men of Babylon, Daniel spoke to him with wisdom and tact* asking him, *'Why did the king issue such a harsh decree?'* Arioch in turn explained and although the king had accused the wise men of delaying tactics, *Daniel went in to the king and asked for time, so that he might interpret the dream for him.*

Having gained the necessary time, Daniel approached his friends, *Hananiah, Mishael and Azariah.* He *explained the matter* to them, urging them to pray with him and to *plead for mercy from the God in heaven concerning this mystery.* In other words, Daniel urged them to pray with him and to beg Yahweh to act according to his nature, that is, to give enlightenment and to act in mercy towards his people. Yahweh intervened as he had done in chapter 1. *During the night the mystery was revealed to Daniel in a vision.*

(b) Daniel's Hymn of Praise (2:20-23)

At this point there is a divergence from the story proper as Daniel's hymn of praise to the God of heaven is recounted. There are two important aspects of God's character that are demonstrated in the hymn. First, as we shall see time and time again through the book of Daniel, God is a sovereign God. He is the one who *changes times and seasons;* who *sets up kings and deposes them.* This leads to the second point. Because he is sovereign and has control of history he is able to reveal the processes of history and what lie behind them. He *reveals deep and hidden things; he knows what lies in darkness, and light dwells with him.* He is the one whom Daniel can *thank and praise* because he has given *wisdom and power.*

In the Bible, history is not determined by impersonal forces at work in the world which need to be divined or otherwise ascertained. Rather, history is determined by a personal God who reveals. God's control over history and therefore his ability to reveal its future are two things fundamental to the character of God. They are the very things that determine and validate God's claim to be God. He alone is God because he can reveal the future (cf Isaiah 41:21-29).

(c) *Nebuchadnezzar's Dream (2:24-35)*

Armed with revelation from God, *Daniel went to Arioch. . . and said to him, 'Do not execute the wise men of Babylon. Take me to the king, and I will interpret his dream for him.'* Arioch obliged. He took Daniel to the king and reported to him that, *'I have found a man among the exiles from Judah who can tell the king what his dream means.'* The lives of the Israelite and the Babylonian wise men were spared, for Daniel was able to tell the king what he saw in his *dream and interpret it.*

Nebuchadnezzar's dream was a terrifying one of a massive colossus out in the sand: *enormous, dazzling* in beauty and *awesome in appearance,* with *head . . . made of pure gold, chest and arms of silver . . . belly and thighs of bronze, legs of iron and feet of iron* and *baked clay.* Although the statue progressed in strength and durability from the head as far as the legs, it decreased in splendour and finally rested on feet of fragile baked clay and iron. The structure was unstable and numbered in its days. However instability was not the cause of its downfall.

As Nebuchadnezzar had dreamed and looked on, he saw *a rock . . . cut out* without the assistance of any *human hands.* It was hurled at the statue, hitting it with force at its fragile base of *iron and clay,* smashing the feet and then the legs, thighs, belly, arms, chest and head. The statue became like *chaff on a threshing floor in the summer,* carried away by the *wind* so that before long no *trace* could be found. Under the impact of the rock the great and magnificent statue was pulverised into fine, light dust while *the rock that struck the statue became a huge mountain and filled the whole earth.*

We have no idea whether Nebuchadnezzar recognised the young man who had stood before him some years earlier and performed ten times better than his other magicians, enchanters and wise men, but there is no doubt that he recognised the dream. Every detail was correct. Belteshazzar had done what the other astrologers had said was impossible. They were convinced that there was *no one* who could *reveal it to the king except the gods, and they do not live among men* (verse 11). Since no one had known it, Nebuchadnezzar could only conclude that Daniel must have got it from its source, the gods themselves. He may have puzzled was it possible that the gods did dwell with human beings? In reality the source of the dream and its interpretation was from the one true God himself.

4. Nebuchadnezzar: Appointed, Opposed And Destroyed (2:36-49)

Daniel immediately proceeded to interpret the dream and to be brutally frank with Nebuchadnezzar, refusing to hide its meaning: *'You, O king, are the king of kings'*.

Nebuchadnezzar was the *head of gold*. His kingdom would go through its development in history and give place to three or four kingdoms, each of which would be impressive in its own right. The end would then come. This end would not come through the sheer collapse of the feet of clay under the immense pressure, but because these man-made kingdoms stood in the way of another God-designed kingdom and must therefore be removed. The man-made kingdoms of Nebuchadnezzar and those who would follow him would be rocked and shattered by the onslaught of a new kingdom carved out of a mountain. *The God of heaven will set up a kingdom that will never be destroyed, nor will it be left to another people. It will crush all those kingdoms and bring them to an end, but it will itself endure forever. This is the meaning of the vision of the rock cut out of a mountain but not by human hands.*

Daniel made things clear: the dream was a revelation from the great God about *what will take place in the future*. The dream was *true* and *the interpretation . . . trustworthy*. In all likelihood the king didn't need to hear such words from

Daniel. He had heard this man relate a dream which no one else had ever heard and which he himself could not remember. He had heard the interpretation and knew that the dream was true and the interpretation faithful and trustworthy. Surely the gods had visited the earth in this man!

The great and devout Nebuchadnezzar was faced with incontrovertible evidence. He did what all devout men do in the presence of deity or the messenger of a deity, he *fell prostrate* on the ground in *honour* and respect, *and ordered that an offering and incense be presented to him.* He honoured the man through gifts and promotions, placing *Daniel in a high position* and lavishing *many gifts on him.* He also, *at Daniel's request* appointed *Shadrach, Meshach and Abednego administrators over the province of Babylon, while Daniel himself remained at the royal court.* More than this, Nebuchadnezzar honoured the God of Daniel, *the God of gods, Lord of kings* and *revealer of mysteries.*

5. Reflecting On The Dreams Of Kings

(a) The Battlefield Of The Gods

There are three crucial comments regarding the gods and their ability to reveal mysteries that stood out in the chapter. The first one came from the astrologers in verse 11 when they said, *'What the king asks is too difficult. No one can reveal the dream to the king except the gods, and they do not live among men.'*

The second came from Daniel's own mouth. In the middle of the chapter, after the dream and its interpretation had been revealed to him and his friends he said to Nebuchadnezzar: *'No wise man, enchanter, magician or diviner can explain to the king the mystery he has asked about, but there is a God in heaven who reveals mysteries. He has shown King Nebuchadnezzar what will happen in days to come.'*

The third came from the mouth of the king at the end of the whole episode where he said, *'Surely your God is the God of gods and the Lord of kings and a revealer of mysteries, for you were able to reveal this mystery.'*

It was obvious from the first day in Babylon that Daniel and his fellow Jews were there because God wanted them there (cf Daniel 1:2) and that he was in some way God's representative, pitted against the Chaldeans and Babylonian wise men. These wise men represented the best in ancient wisdom and learning while he represented a view of wisdom which recognised Yahweh as the source and beginning of all wisdom. Daniel and his friends were therefore caught up in a conflict of two kingdoms or world views.

However, what was said in the three statements went further than just a conflict between Daniel and the Chaldeans or between two different world views. What was being said in the three statements was that while the gods of Babylon could not reveal mysteries, the same can not be said for the God of Israel. He is a revealer of mysteries and superior to the pagan gods. In Nebuchadnezzar's own words, Yahweh was *the God of gods* (2:47).

The real contest in Babylon was therefore not just between Israelite men and Babylonian kings, nor was it just between Israelite wisdom and Babylonian wisdom or between a kingdom-of-God world view and kingdom-of-man world view. The real contest was between the God of Israel and the gods of the nations. God was proclaiming himself to be the victor when Daniel gave Nebuchadnezzar the dream and its interpretation. He was not dead and could take on the gods of Babylon and defeat them. Such victory is inevitable because he alone is God. He alone controls history and he alone reveals mysteries.

In some ways God was asserting his sovereignty over his world through these incidents. Although the conquest, looting, and sacking of Jerusalem by the Babylonians made it look as though God was out of control and had been defeated, the incidents in the life of Daniel and the lives of others like him in Babylonia were saying the opposite. God was still alive, still in control, and still able to vanquish any so-called god or representative of any so-called god.

The implications are clear in our own day. In our jobs, studies, watching of television, and relationships with each other we too are pitted against the representatives of a world view opposed to God's world view. We are caught up in the conflict between two kingdoms. It does not stop there. In us God is at war, engaged in cosmic conflict, taking on the false gods of this world and showing them up as counterfeit.

This is so especially when we preach the gospel. God is at work as we share the good news about Jesus with our friends and contacts. As people respond and accept Jesus, God is saying that he is still alive. He is still in control and still able to vanquish any so-called god, and still able to turn people away from idols to serve a true and living God (1 Thessalonians 1:9).

It is also the case when we live godly lives. As we make choices to turn away from ungodly conduct in our relationships or cheating in our studies or lying and deceiving in our work, God is asserting his sovereignty over his world. He is saying to his world that he can and will win the war in which he is engaged. Our victory over sin, the world, the flesh, and the devil is the continuance of the victory which was won by Jesus on the cross and which will be consummated at the end of the world.

(b) An Accessible God

This chapter also shows up an essential difference between the gods the Babylonians worshipped and the God Daniel worshipped. By their admission the Babylonians worshipped gods who were inaccessible, who 'do not live among men'.

Daniel's God was different and this incident clearly illustrated that difference. Instead of being inaccessible, Yahweh is one *who gives wisdom to the wise and knowledge to the discerning* (2:21). Daniel's God was not a hidden God, but an accessible, revealing, active God.

The God of the Bible is constantly acting and speaking to the people of his world. He does so because he is a God who loves relationships and seeks relationship with those whom he has made. Psalm 19 is a great example of this biblical truth as it celebrates in song God's revelation of himself in creation (verses 1-6) and in Scripture (verses 7-11).

Of course the place where we saw God most visibly going out of his way to communicate with his world was in the life, death, resurrection, and ascension of Jesus. Whereas God had clearly spoken often before, in Jesus he spoke in a crystal clear way, communicating his commitment to his world and involvement in it while also proving his accessibility (cf Hebrews 1.1-3). In Jesus we saw God saying: 'I can be found and I am available to all!' In Jesus God was truly 'dwelling with men' (John 1:14; John 14:5-11).

This revelation of God in Jesus is recorded for us in the Scriptures. For this reason the equivalent of Daniel's praying for the dream to be revealed and for God to give an understanding of it, is our praying that God will give us understanding and enlightenment in our reading of the Scriptures. We must read our Bibles praying that God will be at work in us so that we rightly interpret them.

(c) God And Human Kingdoms

(i)   Human rule as God-given

The dream figure in this chapter is tantalising and while Daniel and his readers may have been tempted to try and work out just what kingdoms were represented by the arms, breast, belly, thighs, legs and feet, (and there has been no end of calculation), this is not the most fundamental point that comes from the dream and its interpretation. The fundamental point comes from noticing the contrasting portrayals of Nebuchadnezzar as they were found in the dream. On the one side Nebuchadnezzar was portrayed in language reminiscent of that used in Genesis 1:28, where Adam was told:

> Be fruitful and increase in number; fill the earth and subdue it. Rule over the fish of the sea and the birds of the air and over every living creature that moves on the ground. (Genesis 1:28)

In the interpretation of the dream God had told Daniel to say of Nebuchadnezzar

> *The God of heaven has given you dominion and power and might and glory; in your hands he has placed mankind and the beasts of the field and the birds of the air. Wherever they live, he has made you ruler over them all.'*
> (Daniel 2:37-8; cf Jeremiah 27:4-7)

The point is that just as Adam was called by God to exercise the rule of God, so Nebuchadnezzar was called by God to exercise the rule of God. Just as Adam had power over the beasts of the field and the birds of the air, so Nebuchadnezzar had been given power. Nebuchadnezzar was God's appointed ruler. His rule was God-given and therefore to submit to the rule of Nebuchadnezzar was to submit to God himself. The implication for Daniel personally was that rather than resisting Nebuchadnezzar or planning his overthrow, he should give allegiance and honour to Nebuchadnezzar, knowing that as he did he was giving allegiance and honour to God.

As Christians we know this well from our New Testaments. Passages such as Matthew 17:24-27; 22:15-22; Romans 13 and 1 Peter 2:13-17 suggest that God has placed governments in our world and given them his rule to exercise. We are called to submit to such authorities when they demand our obedience. This is so whether they ask us to pay taxes, keep road rules, or not infringe copyright on books, videos, tapes or computer software. Unfortunately we Christians do not always stand out in this area. More often than not we flout the rules of our governments and legislators, inventing rationalisations for our illegal activities and metaphorically shaking our fist at them rather than submitting to them for what they are, the representatives of God.

Of course there may be times in our lives when a higher command from God may contradict the command from an earthly ruler. Here we have no choice. We must obey God rather than men (cf Daniel, Shadrach, Meshach and Abednego in Daniel 3 and 6 and the disciples in Acts 4:18-20 and 5:27-32). This aside, the facts are that most of us have more to learn in the area of civil obedience than we have in the area of civil disobedience.

(ii) Human rule as idolatry

The other side was there also. While Daniel may have noticed the allusions to Genesis 1 and the mandate given to Adam in the message he delivered to Nebuchadnezzar, he also noticed the clear implication of the dream. Nebuchadnezzar's rule was represented as a huge image, an idol, the ultimate in human pretensions to power, sovereignty and beauty. It had to be thrown down by God.

The point is clear: Nebuchadnezzar and the nations that followed him had been given dominion over God's world, to rule it as God's representatives. However, Nebuchadnezzar was no different from Adam or any of the kings of Israel. In the long run his kingdom was made by human hands. Kingdoms such as Nebuchadnezzar's may be brilliant in splendour yet they all rest on feet which are of iron mixed with clay. This base on which all human kingdoms rest shows their real character which God will further demonstrate when he carves out his kingdom. Such a kingdom will not be man-made, constructed with human hands. It will be one that will be solid and lasting, never shaken, breaking into the midst of world affairs with irresistible and ever growing power. This kingdom of God would finally establish itself without rival and without opposition.

Daniel knew from where that kingdom would come. He knew of only one mountain from which God would carve out a kingdom. It was the mountain on which Zion stood, the city of David. As Daniel daily served his God-appointed human king, he no doubt thanked God for this comment at the end of the dream interpretation. A comment which might never be understood by Nebuchadnezzar but which was understood by him. Daniel could look forward to, pray for and long to greet the coming of that kingdom of God when God would be recognised as the only true and living God, who alone was God of Gods and Lord of kings.

6. Postscript to Daniel 2

As Daniel grew older he too dreamed. Like Nebuchadnezzar, he craved interpretation and explanation, and received it from the messengers of God. Like Nebuchadnezzar there were things in his dreams of which he longed to understand more, but could not. Most particularly he longed to understand more about the coming kingdom of God. Just when would it arrive? How would it come? What events would herald its emergence? Like the prophets before him who spoke of the grace that was to come, he searched intently and earnestly. He tried to find out the time and circumstances to which the Spirit in them was pointing when he predicted the sufferings and glory to come (cf 1 Peter 1:10-12).

Years later it did begin to happen. God began steadily to carve out a kingdom made without hands. He matched a reluctant priest and a barren woman and gave them a child who grew into a wild and reclusive man whose mouth spilled words of fire and imminent judgment whenever it opened. From this most unlikely source the announcement of the coming of the kingdom of God rang out across the hills and valleys of Palestine,

Repent, for the kingdom of heaven is near (Matthew 3:2)

And again,

I baptise you with water for repentance. But after me will come one who is more powerful than I, whose sandals I am not fit to carry. He will baptise you with the Holy Spirit and with fire. His winnowing fork is in his hand, and he will clear his threshing floor, gathering his wheat into the barn and burning up the chaff with unquenchable fire. (Matthew 3:11-12)

This John the Baptist spoke in the same vein as Daniel. He spoke of a coming kingdom of God that would put an end to all the kingdoms that men and women had built. He spoke about Jesus in whom God would set up a kingdom made without hands. In Jesus the world did see God at work, breaking into history and setting up a kingdom of Jewish and Davidic stock. Today we continue to see the kingdom of God breaking into history, altering it and bringing salvation and judgment in its path. In Jesus, God is hurling the rock at the feet of the kingdoms of men as he revealed he would in the shadow world of Nebuchadnezzar's dream.

FOR STUDY, DISCUSSION AND PRAYER

1.   What do verses 11-12, 27-28, and 47 tell us about the primary point of this chapter?

2.   Who are the people who have authority over you? How should we respond to human authorities in our world (Daniel 2; Jeremiah 27:1-7; Romans 13:1-7; Matthew 22:15-22; cf Acts 4 and 5)?

3.   How does Daniel respond to the impossible odds stacked against him? On what basis does he make his response?

4.   Where do you find yourself caught up in conflict between God's kingdom and the kingdoms of this world? How should we react and how can we help and support each other in this conflict?

8

Understanding The Kingdom Of God (I)

One of the important facets of the book of Daniel that travels down to our own day with great force and significance is its teaching about the kingdom of God. So much of the book of Daniel is taken up with talking about the kingdom of God that we will find our picture of it gradually grow as we read on in the book and begin to understand it. However, in order to grasp what he is saying, we need to understand some of the background that lies behind the picture of the kingdom it portrays.

1. The Creator King

The Old Testament Scriptures with which Daniel was familiar proclaimed God to be the Creator of the world and therefore its King. They did so by taking the word 'king' and applying it to God and by talking about God's exercise of kingly functions. For example:

Clap your hands, all you nations; shout to God with cries of joy. How awesome is the Lord Most High, the great King over all the earth!

For God is the King of all the earth; sing to him a psalm of praise. God reigns over the nations; God is seated on his holy throne. The nobles of the nations assemble as the people of the God of Abraham, for the Kings of the earth belong to God; he is greatly exalted. (Psalm 47:1-2; 7-9; cf. Psalm 103:19; 145:10-13)

This is the first building block in our understanding of the kingdom of God as presented in the Old Testament

- As Creator of the world, God is its one true King.

In Daniel 2 we have seen this idea come to the fore. Daniel's God was proclaimed to be *the God of gods and the Lord of kings* (verse 47). He was the one who gave human kingship to human beings, and by that showed he was King over all kings (verses 36-38).

2. A God With A Purpose

Daniel also knew from the Old Testament Scriptures that God's kingship was a purposive kingship. The God of the Old Testament was not a king who sat on a throne waiting for the next crisis to come before developing a policy and then acting on it. Nor was he a king who started something but did not know how it would develop in the future. Rather, he was the God who began history and was purposively bringing it to an end, overseeing each intimate detail of its progress. This can be seen in such crucial events as the calling of Abraham, the exile of the Israelites in Babylon, their rescue out of Babylon and subsequent entry into the promised land, and the fulfilment of the promises under David and Solomon. The God of the Old Testament was the Lord and King of history who was at work in it to cause a situation where the whole world would recognise and worship him as King. Again, the Scriptures that speak about this are many and include:

This is what the Lord says – Israel's King and redeemer, the Lord Almighty: I am the first and I am the last; apart from me there is no God. Who is like me? Let him proclaim it. Let him declare and lay out before me what has happened since I established my ancient people, and what is yet to come – yes, let him foretell what will come. Do not tremble, do not be afraid. Did I not proclaim this and foretell it long ago? You are my witnesses. Is there any God beside me? No, there is no other Rock; I know not one. (Isaiah 44:6-8)

In that day the Lord will punish the powers in the heavens above and the kings on the earth below. They will be herded together like prisoners bound in a dungeon; they will be shut up in prison and punished for many days. The moon will be abashed, the sun ashamed; for the Almighty will reign on Mount Zion and in Jerusalem, and before its elders, gloriously. (Isaiah 24:21-23)

This is the second building block in our understanding of the kingdom of God in the Old Testament:

- The kingship of God is headed toward a goal: the world living under God as King and the end of all rivals to his kingship.

Again, Daniel 2 is full of this idea. God gave authority to human rulers, but their rule was fragile, fragmentary and standing on feet of clay. He was therefore at work to bring human rule to an end, to judge all human kingdoms and to establish his kingdom as the only kingdom.

Daniel must have been very aware of this as he looked back on the prophecies of such great ones as Isaiah and Jeremiah who had so accurately laid out God's plan for his people before the destruction of Jerusalem. His God was the King and Lord of history, working towards a specific goal for history and overseeing its progress. What is more, he was dwelling in Babylon because *the Lord delivered Jehoiakim, King of Judah, into the hands of Nebuchadnezzar, king of Babylon* (1:2).

3. The God Who Delegates

There is a third element of the Old Testament's teaching on the kingdom of God which also surfaces in Daniel 2. It was the fact that God delegated his kingship to human beings.

In the ancient world an image of a god or a king was considered to represent the god or king. Therefore, if a king built a statue over a particular area he did so to announce his dominion over the area in which it was built. In a sense the statue represented him and his rule.

Something like this can be seen in Genesis 1 and Psalm 8. In Genesis 1:27f human beings were set in the midst of the rest of creation as God's representation. This is evidence that God was the Lord or King over all creation.

This is not all. They were also God's stewards, or vice-regents, called to exercise God's rule over the lower orders of creation. This was made clear in Genesis 1, where as soon as man was called *the image of God*, he was urged to exercise sovereignty over the rest of creation. He was to *fill the earth and subdue it and rule over the fish of the sea and the birds of the air and over every living creature that moves on the ground*. The same was so in Psalm 8 – God had made man *ruler over the works of his hands, putting everything under his feet*. Human beings were created in God's image, they were kings and queens over nature and were to rule the world on God's behalf.

As the Bible progresses, it becomes evident that some people exercise the rule of God over other human beings as well as over other living creatures. This was especially so with kings, who represent human beings as a whole. In them the role of exercising the rule of God over his world was particularly concentrated.

This is the third building block in our understanding of the kingdom of God:

- God delegates his kingship to human beings.

As we have seen above, this idea is clear in Daniel 2. Nebuchadnezzar was spoken of in language that calls Genesis 1:27f to mind and emphasises Nebuchadnezzar's crucial role and responsibility. Daniel told Nebuchadnezzar that *'the God of heaven has given you dominion and power and might and glory; in your hands he has placed mankind and the beasts of the field and the birds of the air. Wherever they live, he has made you ruler over them all.'*

4. Kingdom Building Blocks

These are the first three building blocks in our understanding of the kingdom of God in the Old Testament.

As we continue to watch and listen to Daniel and to God at work through him we will continue to build up an even fuller understanding of the kingdom of God and of God's purpose in his world. However, we shall summarise what the book of Daniel has taught us to this point.

5. Living with the Kingship of God

(a) Giving Honour Where Honour Is Due

Our God is the King of all the earth. This is a word to us which has a double edge to it. The first edge is one that cuts many of us down to the bone. It warns us that if God is King then he has appointed various people in positions of authority and demands that we give them our devotion, honour and loyalty. As we have seen, this means obeying their laws (except those that transgress God's higher laws, especially that of gospel preaching), paying their taxes, respecting them and the like.

The corollary of this is that God does not call us to overthrow pagan kingdoms and to establish the kingdom through violence or even to be revolutionaries for him. On the contrary, he calls us to act as servants of his appointed rulers of this world.

(b) God's Coming Kingdom

The second way in which the kingship of God has impact on us is one with which we are more familiar. If God is King then he has a day when he will bring an end to all the kingdoms of men and a time when only his kingdom, which cannot be shaken, will remain. Jesus' coming into the world brought this kingdom into existence. Although it is still very much like a mustard seed the day will come when the kingdom will be consummated and it will fill the whole earth.

This is a word that speaks to any who think that utopia, reality, or the kingdom of God can be found with human endeavour. It warns that any and every system that closes itself to the living influence of God the King will face darkness, dismay and the anger of God. The kingdom of God will grow and gather momentum and will blow away all which cannot be incorporated within it. Independent kingdoms and independent people will be as chaff that the wind sweeps away from the threshing floor in summer (Daniel 2:35).

This is great news to us when we look around the world at the dictators and despots who seem to rule the world with little of the compassion, mercy and justice which characterises the rule of God. It is great news because it says that their day will come. God has a day when he will punish the arrogance of man and his attempts to build kingdoms opposing his kingdom (cf Isaiah 2:9-22; Revelation 18).

It is not such good news when we look at our own lives. Unfortunately we too are often found pursuing our own little kingdoms. We do this in our work places, families, relationships, churches, parachurch organisations and the like. These little 'people-made' kingdoms consume us, direct and captivate us during our waking (and dreaming!) hours. Too often our rule in them is autonomous. It is not subject to the kingship of Jesus and not modelled on his kingly rule of compassion, mercy, justice and self giving. God's word comes to us from Daniel 2 and tells us that our day will also come. God has a day when he will punish our arrogance and our attempts to build kingdoms opposing his kingdom (cf. Isaiah 2:9ff; Revelation 18).

(c) Living In Two Kingdoms

(i) Proclamation

The book of Daniel and the rest of the Bible calls us to live as people who belong to two kingdoms. One is faulty and temporary, but nevertheless God-appointed. Another is perfect and eternal and will never be shaken. We live as people of these two kingdoms by knowing that a time will come when God will establish his kingdom and by announcing, as Daniel did, the eternal kingship of God and his coming judgment on those who will not bow to his rule. We are to do what Daniel, the prophets, John the Baptist and Jesus did. We are to announce in a good clear voice, 'Repent, for the kingdom of God is at hand.'

(ii) Prayer in the fellowship of God's people

Daniel also shouts loudly across the centuries to us on the issue of living in two kingdoms. We hear his clear voice echoing as he modeled life in two kingdoms. When we find ourselves asking, 'As God's person, what do I do when I find myself confronted with some of the more nasty consequences of living in the kingdoms of men?' We hear Daniel cry back, 'Godly people pray and seek the mercy and compassion of God the King and sovereign Lord. They ask him for rescue and they ask him for revelation and help. Life committed to the kingdom of God but lived in the kingdom of man can be successful only when the people of God together cast themselves on their God.'

There are not many of us who can confront the world alone as it seeks to overpower us and seduce us. Not many of God's people have managed to serve God alone in the world and maintain integrity and faithfulness to clear kingdom values without compromise. There are only a few who have stood alone and shouted out the word of repentance and judgment to a world radically opposed to God and his kingdom. But God did not intend us to stand alone! He intended that we do these things in the fellowship of others, binding us together in churches and fellowship groups for this purpose.

It does not matter whether we are the theologian trying to grapple with the true meaning of the Scriptures, the business-person trying to act in a godly manner in his dealings with his company and fellow workers, the housewife who is struggling to keep her temper with children who give her no peace, the pastor grappling with dilemmas thrown up by congregational life, or the student planning how to bring the gospel to a pagan campus. God did not intend us to be alone but that we support each other in prayer. Perhaps if we did our theologians would not wander from the truth, our ministers might preach more boldly, our business-people retain the cutting edge of their faith, our fathers and mothers bring up godly children, and our students plan more effectively. If we spent time supporting each other then maybe we would not be so ungodly in our conduct and so weak in our speech.

Daniel teaches us to pray. He prayed and God granted such success that the king of kings paid homage to Daniel, the servant of the Most High, the one in whom the Spirit of God so evidently dwelt.

(d) Reaching for Reality

Finally, Daniel warns us that in this chapter we have touched reality. Reality is not so much about building houses, paying off mortgages, getting promotions, growing churches, or making money. Reality is about a God who is King and who is inexorably bringing in his kingdom made without hands. Reality is about that day when God will send his Crown Prince.

FOR STUDY, DISCUSSION AND PRAYER

1. Read Psalms 2 and 8. What do these Psalms teach about:
    God's kingship?

    The role of humans in relationship to God's kingship and his creation?

2. Discuss ways in which your prayer and support for each other and other Christians could be improved.

3. Work out a plan for improving the prayer life of your group and implement it over the next few meetings together.

4. If you have access to it, examine the tract 'Two Ways To Live'. How does it use the idea of the kingdom of God to present the gospel?

9

When The Heat's Turned On 3:1-18

1. Jews in Babylon

(a) Filled with Awe

The city of Babylon evoked a variety of emotions from the Jews who experienced it. It would undoubtedly have been met with awe by the Jerusalem Jews from the very first time they had been dragged in chains through the massive Ishtar Gate in a spectacular victory parade. The huge Processional Way which led down through the centre of the city was paved with coloured stones from Lebanon, red breccia, and limestone. Nine hundred metres of walls lined the roadway with their enamelled bricks depicting dragons and bulls (representing local deities) ranged in alternate rows. Babylon was a city like no other.

(b) Revolted

Simultaneously the city would have revolted them and caused deep offence. The whole city held up pagan gods and pagan kings as sovereign and victorious. Even the paving stones and street names shouted out against the King of heaven. Paving stones proclaimed, 'I Nebuchadnezzar, king of Babylon, paved this road with mountain stone for the procession of Marduk, my lord. May Marduk my lord grant me eternal life.' Street names broadcasted that 'Adad has guarded the life of the people'. Jews believed in only one God, Yahweh, and in the necessity of humility before his sovereignty. They could not help being offended and disturbed.

(c) Ashamed

A Jew in Babylon must also have felt shame. Yahweh wanted his nation to be living in the land he had promised Abraham, worshipping the God of Abraham, Isaac and Jacob in a temple constructed and overseen by a king descended from David. Yet the nation had failed. They heard the promises but did not grasp the vision and live by it. They had rejected it and the God who had promised it so they experienced his judgment in exile. Instead of celebrating the presence of God in a temple in Jerusalem they were grimacing at pagan temples that held within them the gold vessels of God's temple in Jerusalem. In the place of a king descended from David they were captives of the pagan king Nebuchadnezzar. God's temple was destroyed. His nation ravaged, his glory desecrated and his name profaned among the nations. There was a lot of which to be ashamed.

(d) Scared

As the Jews had been dragged across the desert to exile they must have been in great fear, not knowing what fate awaited them. Upon arriving in Babylon, however, their fears were found to have been far too extravagant. True, there had been brutality, torture and hardship. They did not have absolute freedom and occasionally found themselves without enough to eke out a livelihood. Nevertheless, circumstances were not that bad. The nation had not been dispersed, as the northern tribes had been when conquered by Assyria. Instead, they were in a settlement with their own people (cf Ezekiel 3:15; Ezra 2:59; 8:17). Although not totally free, they were not prisoners either. They were allowed to build houses, engage in agriculture (cf Jeremiah 29:5f), and earn a living in any way they could. There was right of assembly and room to maintain some sort of community life (cf Ezekiel 8:1; 14:1; 33:30f). Jeremiah's advice was timely and necessary.

> This is what the Lord Almighty, the God of Israel, says to all those I carried into exile from Jerusalem to Babylon: 'Build houses and settle down; plant gardens and eat what they produce. Marry and have sons and daughters; find wives for your sons and give your daughters in marriage, so that they too may have sons and daughters. Increase in number there; do not decrease. Also, seek the peace and prosperity of the city to which I have carried you in exile. Pray to the Lord for it, because if it prospers, you too will prosper.' (Jeremiah 29:4-7)

2. It Was Hard Being A Jew In Babylon

However, although life was not as bad as expected, it was still difficult being a Jew. It was especially difficult being a Jew in authority. This is made clear in chapter 3 of Daniel. It is recorded that at some time in his career, *King Nebuchadnezzar made an image of gold, ninety feet high and nine feet wide, and set it up on the plain of Dura in the province of Babylon. He then summoned the satraps, prefects, governors, advisers, treasurers, judges, magistrates and all the other provincial officials to come to the dedication of the image he had set up.*

Having gathered them Nebuchadnezzar's herald loudly proclaimed, *'This is what you are commanded to do, O peoples, nations and men of every language: As soon as you hear the sound of the horn, flute, zither, lyre, harp, pipes and all kinds of music, you must fall down and worship the image of gold that King Nebuchadnezzar has set up. Whoever does not fall down and worship will immediately be thrown into a blazing furnace.'*

(a) No!

Nebuchadnezzar's statue on the plain was grotesquely tall and plated with gold. The dimensions were startling and fitted the grandeur of his position and personality. The passage does not say exactly what the statue was or what it was that motivated him to erect it and nor did it matter. It was clear to good Jews that it was pagan and that it was raised as a challenge to their God. It was also obvious to Shadrach, Meshach and Abednego that they could have no part of it or of the ritual surrounding it. They could not bow down before it. To fall prostrate before it would be tantamount to recognising Nebuchadnezzar and his gods. Again the young men said 'No!'.

(b) Exposed!

This time there was no shortage of people willing to notice the conscientious objection of the Jews. *Some astrologers came forward and denounced the Jews.* They reminded the king of his decree and of his warning that *whoever does not fall down and worship will be thrown into a blazing furnace* and reported that *'There are some Jews whom you have set over the affairs of the province of Babylon – Shadrach, Meshach and Abednego – who pay no attention to you, O king. They neither serve your gods nor worship the image of gold you have set up.'*

The report was designed to cause affront to Nebuchadnezzar. The words *you, your, you* stress that these men were not in revolt against a decree, but a person. Their act of political defiance was an act of personal defiance against Nebuchadnezzar.

As we saw when we looked at chapter 1, Jews had no 'in principle' objections to living in a pagan environment. Their God was God in Babylon as well as in the stretch of land between Dan and Beersheba. This did not make living with pagans easy. Jews were fundamentally different to others in their world. They worshipped one God rather than the multitude of gods that other nations worshipped and because of their monotheism they were often suspected and hated. People did not know what to do with them and often thought of them almost as atheists because of their refusal to worship a variety of gods as others did. As if this was not enough, they despised images and detested any kind of idol. Jews were considered an incredibly odd group of people, removed from the rest of humanity because of their beliefs and practices.

This meant that while *all the peoples, nations and men of every language who heard the sound of the horn, flute, zither, lyre, harp and all kinds of music* had no great trouble in falling down and worshipping *the image of gold that King Nebuchadnezzar had set up,* a loyal Jew could not.

The added difficulty for Shadrach, Meshach and Abednego was that their positions of authority in Nebuchadnezzar's kingdom made them visible to all. People knew what they did and did not do, and their loyalty to God and adherence to their religion did not fail to be visible. They were therefore vulnerable. If they did well in their jobs then they became extremely vulnerable and if someone did not like them or wanted their position, then it was easy to trap them. All that had to be done was to manufacture or report any situations where their choice for God resulted in a choice against the king. This story and the one in chapter 6 indicate that Daniel, Shadrach, Meshach and Abednego made a name for themselves very early on and as a result were surrounded by enemies. People around them were jealous and were continually planning how they might be removed from positions of power.

Nebuchadnezzar was *furious with rage.* He *summoned* the men, asking if the charges were *true,* and giving them a last opportunity to change their minds. He said to them, *'Now when you hear the sound of the horn, flute, zither, lyre, harp, pipes and all kinds of music, if you are ready to fall down and worship the image I made, very good. But if you do not worship it, you will be thrown immediately into a blazing furnace. Then what god will be able to rescue you from my hand?'*

To understand how the three men reacted to this challenge it is necessary to understand some of the factors that continually influenced them and their fellow Jews in Babylon. Every Jew knew why the nation was in Babylon. Their ancestors were given commandments by God. Chief among these commandments were the first two. The first stated: 'You shall have no other gods before me'. The second declared:

'You shall not make for yourself a graven image, or any likeness of anything that is in heaven above, or that is in the earth beneath, or that is in the water under the earth; you shall not bow down to them or serve them; for I the Lord your God am a jealous God, visiting the iniquity of the fathers upon the children to the third and fourth generation of those who hate me but showing steadfast love to thousands of those who love me and keep my commandments.'

These two commandments formed the core of their faith as well as the core of their sin and consequent judgment. The history of their nation had been played out in terms of their failure to keep these commandments. That is why they were in exile, away from their land and their homes. It was because of their failure in this area they had found themselves away from their great city and its temple. They experienced God's anger and punishment for their sin as he had promised they would if they continued in sin.

It appears that those who saw or heard about the destruction of Jerusalem and the temple were determined that there would not be a repeat of the sins of their ancestors. They were determined to be loyal and obedient to his commandments, agreeing with each other that they would keep these two commandments at any cost.

(c) No Choice Really

As far as Shadrach, Meshach and Abednego were concerned, they had no choice. No matter how many musical instruments were played, they could not *fall down and worship the image* Nebuchadnezzar had made. To bow down and worship would have been to acknowledge another power and sovereignty that needed worship other than Yahweh the great king.

There is a difficulty in the Hebrew meaning of verses 17 and 18. This difficulty can be seen in the various English translations. The best translation appears to be the one which stresses the whole idea of God's existence, such as that given in the New English Bible, which translates the text in the following manner:

> *If there is a God who is able to save us from the blazing furnace, it is our God whom we serve, and he will save us from your power, O king; but if not, be it known that we will neither serve your god nor worship the golden image that you have set up.*

Since Nebuchadnezzar had already asked whether there was a god who can rescue, this translation fits the context. Shadrach, Meshach and Abednego put the challenge to Nebuchadnezzar. If there is such a God, then he is the one they worship and he will rescue them. Even if he does not rescue them, they will not worship Nebuchadnezzar's golden image.

John Goldingay has captured the same idea in his translation of the passage (*Daniel*, Word Bible Commentary, 1989, p 64):

> *O Nebuchadnezzar, we do not need to make any response regarding this. If our God, whom we honour, exists, he is able to rescue us from the red – hot blazing furnace, and he will rescue us from your power, your majesty. Even if he should not, your majesty may be assured that we are not going to honour your gods or bow down to the gold statue which you have set up.*

It was not that Shadrach, Meshach and Abednego doubted God's existence, but that the king doubted it. He had demonstrated his doubt that any god existed who could challenge him and his decree. Shadrach, Meshach and Abednego showed their confidence that God was not only able to rescue them, but also that he was going to do it. Nebuchadnezzar had thrown down the gauntlet to God and they were sure that God would act to rescue and by that demonstrate his existence and power. Nevertheless, although they were confident they knew that they could not bind God to act as they predicted. They knew that although they were confident, God remained free. There was a theoretical possibility that he would not respond as expected and rescue them.

FOR STUDY, DISCUSSION AND PRAYER

1. What ideas, habits, and beliefs do modern Christians
    have that (1) bring them into open conflict with those
    around them, or (2) are misunderstood by those
    around them?

2. It can be helpful to split these things into three
    categories:

*   Things we would die for (that is stand for, no matter
    what the cost).

*   Things we would fight for, but not die for.

*   Things we believe in, but would give up without too
    much fuss.

    Categorise each of the things you listed in question 1
    into these groups. Discuss with others why you would
    put each of them into the particular category that you
    did.

3. Spend time praying for Christian people you are
    aware of who are in prominent positions of authority
    either in society or in the church.

10

The Cost of
Discipleship 3:19-30

What Shadrach, Meshach and Abednego did was extremely difficult. In chapter 1 their rebellion had been discrete and hidden from the eyes of the king. In this chapter they were flagrantly disobeying the king and defying him to his face. However, they knew they had to do it and were convinced that it was worth giving up their lives rather than worship a false God (cf Daniel 2:28). Having taken this step they did the only thing remaining. They trusted in God even though they had little hope of rescue.

Their words to Nebuchadnezzar were like a 'red rag to a bull'. He burned with fury. *His attitude toward* Shadrach, Meshach and Abednego *changed* and his anger fuelled his resolve so that he *ordered the furnace to be heated seven times hotter than usual and commanded some of the strongest soldiers in his army to tie them up and throw them into the blazing furnace.*

The soldiers came forward, bound the men and carried them towards the furnace. Fully clothed, *wearing their robes, trousers, turbans and other clothes,* the men *were bound and thrown into the blazing furnace. The king's command was so urgent and the furnace so hot that the flames of the fire killed the soldiers who took* them up.

The writer heightened the tension through vivid descriptions of what the men were wearing, stressing the

74

urgency of the king's command and the heat of the furnace
and its effect on the soldiers. As readers of the Bible we know
that God rescues, especially when he has been challenged and
defied. Somehow we know God will act, but such tension
causes us to ask, when and how?

1. A God Who Is Able

At this point the writer shifted the focus to
Nebuchadnezzar. Although something was obviously
happening in the furnace all that was seen was
Nebuchadnezzar's reaction. The writer revealed that he
*leaped to his feet in amazement and asked his advisers, 'Weren't
there three men that we tied up and threw into the fire?'* The answer
came. *'Certainly, O king.'* The king cried out: *'Look! I see four
men walking around in the fire, unbound and unharmed, and the
fourth looks like a son of the gods.'*

The term 'son of the gods' was probably just a way of saying
something supernatural or something which cannot be
explained. What was to be understood through the presence
of the 'son of the gods' was that somehow God is present with
these men. He had sent help and rescued them as we knew
he would.

*'Nebuchadnezzar then approached the opening of the blazing
furnace and shouted, 'Shadrach, Meshach and Abednego, servants
of the Most High God, come out! Come here!'*

The first thing that was focused on was the worshippers of
the statue on the plain. The *satraps, prefects, governors and royal
advisers* who bowed before a false image *crowded around* to see
the work of the real God.

The focus then shifted to the men. Nebuchadnezzar had
imagined that there was no god in existence who could rescue
the men from his hand (3:15). On the contrary, there was a
God, the God of Shadrach, Meshach and Abednego, who
could so protect his people that *fire* did not harm *their bodies,*

nor singe *a hair of their heads*, nor scorch *their robes*, nor even leave a *smell of fire on them*.

Finally, the focus shifted to the most important person, God. Where the chapter had started with a focus on an earthly king asserting his power, it concluded with the same king acknowledging the power of a greater king and praising him.

> *Praise be to the God of Shadrach, Meshach and Abednego, who has sent his angel and rescued his servants! They trusted in him and defied the king's command and were willing to give up their lives rather than serve or worship any god except their God. Therefore I decree that the people of any nation or language who say anything against the God of Shadrach, Meshach and Abednego be cut into pieces and their houses be turned into piles of rubble, for no other god can save in this way.*

Nevertheless, although Nebuchadnezzar had seen the power of the great king at work, although he had met the God who is able to *save in this way*, he was still keen on asserting his own sovereignty and on controlling the religious attitudes of his subjects by force. He decreed that *the people of any nation or language who say anything against the God of Shadrach, Meshach and Abednego be cut into pieces and their houses be turned into piles of rubble.*

2. A Larger Perspective On The Chapter

(a) An Alternative To The One God

A helpful insight to this chapter can be gained by remembering that it was probably designed to be read aloud, with the reader knowing the story and inserting his own emphasis on various parts of the story to heighten its drama.

Reading the passage aloud causes various facets to stand out. An element of humour is introduced by the constant repetition of the names of the Babylonian officials, the musical instruments, the words *'the image* [of gold] *Nebuchadnezzar had set up'*, and the names of the three Jews, coupled with the references to the heat of the fire, the clothes of the three Jews, and the fate of those who dragged them to the furnace. You can almost imagine Jews sitting in a synagogue hearing the passage read out and laughing among themselves as they conjured up in their minds a picture of the great ones of the Babylonian world bowing and scraping in unison to the sound of music.

Of course, mocking idolatry and polytheism were not new to Jews. There is a fine example in Isaiah 44 where Isaiah systematically attacked idolatry and at the same time mocked those who used it.

All who make idols are nothing, and the things they treasure are worthless. Those who speak up for them are blind; they are ignorant, to their own shame. Who shapes a god and casts an idol, which can profit him nothing? He and his kind will be put to shame; craftsmen are nothing but men. Let them all come together and take their stand; they will be brought down to terror and infamy.

The blacksmith takes a tool and works with it in the coals; he shapes an idol with hammers, he forges it with the might of his arm. He gets hungry and loses his strength; he drinks no water and grows faint. The carpenter measures with a line and makes an outline with a marker; he roughs it out with chisels and marks it with compasses. He shapes it in the form of man, of man in all his glory, that it may dwell in a shrine. He cut down cedars, or perhaps took a cypress or oak. He let it grow among the trees of the forest, or planted a pine, and the rain made it grow. It is man's fuel for burning; some of it he takes and warms himself, he kindles a fire and bakes bread. But he also fashions a god and worships it; he makes an idol and bows down to it. Half of the wood he burns in the fire; over it he prepares his meal, he roasts his meat and eats his fill. He also warms himself and says, 'Ah! I am warm; I see the fire.' From the rest he makes a god, his idol; he bows down before it and worships. He prays to it and says, 'Save me; you are my god.' They know nothing, they understand nothing; their eyes are plastered over so that they cannot see, and their minds closed so that they cannot understand. No one stops to think, no one has the knowledge or understanding to say, 'Half of it I used for fuel; I even baked bread over its coals, I roasted meat and I ate. Shall I make a detestable thing from what is left? Shall I bow down to a block of wood?' He feeds on ashes, a deluded heart misleads him; he cannot save himself, or say, 'Is not this thing in my right hand a lie?' (Isaiah 44:9-20)

By laughing at polytheism Jewish writers reinforced the stupidity of man-made religion. Such religion in the end has you playing games with a petty tyrant like Nebuchadnezzar. The Scriptures taught Jews that polytheism was stupid, but it was the antics of those like Nebuchadnezzar and his officials that convinced them beyond a shadow of doubt that these Scriptures were right. Knowing the real God they could have nothing to do with such stupidity. They could not bow when the music played.

The point of the passage is clear. It was hard living in Babylon and believing in the true God. Living in Babylon was living in a world opposed to God and his reality. It was living in a world opposed to the people of God.

There were two choices which faced Daniel, Shadrach, Meshach and Abednego in Babylon. They could

It's even harder toly. People are not opposed to God. They are apathetic. They simply don't care!

78

compromise, letting go of God by becoming Babylonians, or they could hang on to God and risk their lives and success. Everything around them pointed to the first alternative as the better choice, however their knowledge of God and reality pointed them towards the only wise alternative. When they looked a bit harder at Babylon and its false religion they knew that there was absolutely no choice. Anything else was not only a denial of truth and of their identity, it was also great foolishness. Paganism is foolishness. The fool says in his heart, 'there is no God' (Psalm 14:1). Belief in God is where reality is found.

(b) The Cost And Glory Of Discipleship

Of course, each of the men would have known that there would be a cost to be paid. Living for God in Babylon would undoubtedly have meant persecution and suffering at sometime. After all, those who desire to live godly lives will be persecuted (2 Timothy 3:12). The incident in the furnace proved to them another great truth which they undoubtedly knew in theory. No matter what happens to the godly, God will be there with them. If we stand with God, he will stand with us. If we disown him, he will disown us (2 Timothy 2:11-13).

At the start, Nebuchadnezzar issued a decree that defied God. At the end he issued another decree that acknowledged the power and reality of the true God and made worship of him legal in Babylon. Shadrach, Meshach and Abednego trusted in God, and refused to obey the king's command. They yielded up their bodies rather than worship a false God. This resulted in God's people being kept safe and in his being glorified and acknowledged by this defiant king.

We must be careful not to misread this chapter. God's rescue of Shadrach, Meshach and Abednego is proof that he does exist and that he is able to rescue. He did not have to come to their rescue. In some cases he does not come to the rescue of his saints. God gives no guarantees about rescuing us from suffering. What he does do is give us guarantees about where he will be when we suffer. He will be with us. That is the point of the fourth figure in the fire. When God's people suffer for God's purpose and God's glory he will never leave them alone.

3. No Choice Really

(a) It Is Hard Being a Christian

It is never easy being a Christian in our world. Being a Christian makes you distinctive. You stand out in the crowd, noticed as different because of your beliefs and practices.

In the area of beliefs, Christians stand out because they believe in God and think that others should too. They are perceived to be bigoted, thinking that they alone have the right understanding of who God is and how to relate to him. Christians believe that other religions have nothing to do with reality and that Jesus is the only way to know the real God. If that were not enough, they cling to a book written over nineteen centuries ago believing that it ought to be the definitive guide for faith and conduct.

Furthermore, Christians are strange in their lifestyle, openly rejecting many practices of those who surround them at university or at work. They spend their time in unusual ways: reading their Bibles, attending church, and going out at night to study the Bible and pray with their friends. Unlike many others in today's world, they respect authority and obey the law and refuse to take revenge on those who are malicious towards them. Cheating in exams or using illegal means to avoid paying tax is considered inappropriate. Christians do not believe in lying to the boss and do believe in the importance of keeping their word. They are not afraid of

acknowledging and confessing any shortcomings or
wrongdoing openly and publicly and do not think that they
are the centre of the universe or that the aim of life is pleasure
and its pursuit. They don't follow commonly accepted
patterns of sexual behaviour or get tied up with the excesses
of their friends in other areas.

On all counts, Christians are odd people, somehow out of
place in the modern world. They are people that threaten
their world by their beliefs and practices and who, by their
words and actions, call their world and the people in it to
stop rebelling and change direction.

(b) But Look At The Alternatives

Christians know why they are the way they are. They have
met God in Jesus and in him have come to know reality. They
know that the world is God's and that the only way to live in
it is in relationship to him. They have found life and its full
meaning in Jesus.

When Christians look around at the world they are
confirmed in their decision to live with and for God because
of the stupidity of the alternatives. Christians stand in
stunned amazement at people who live primarily for their
salary cheques, bowing and scraping to their bosses in the
hope of gaining advancement or prestige. They are
incredulous that someone should live life at the beck and call
of a transitory master, committed to ambitions, careers,
possessions and their own little kingdoms at the cost of a
relationship with God and true, vital, reconciled relationships
with other people. Christians join with their Master in his
immense sorrow that people should spend their lives gaining
the world only to lose their own souls.

(c) There Is Really No Choice

As God's people Christians know that there is nothing as ridiculous as man-made religion, no matter what name it goes by. They know that there is really no choice but to commit themselves to the real God and to the reality that comes through his Son, Jesus. Christians know that they can no longer live as fools, thinking that reality can be found in money, sex, pleasure, possessions, careers, or the finiteness of their minds.

(d) But There Is A Cost To Be Paid For Reality

Christians also realise that opting for reality is costly. They have seen it often in the lives of those who have lived for God before them. Moreover, they have seen it in the life of their Lord. The people of God know that commitment to God and his kingdom places them at odds with the kingdoms of this world. Like Paul they know that 'everyone who desires to live a godly life in Christ Jesus will be persecuted' (see 2 Timothy 3:12). Reality comes with the cold, hard nails of a cross.

Christians hang on to the words of Jesus who said that whoever seeks to save his life shall lose it and that whoever loses his life for the sake of Jesus and the gospel shall save it (Luke 9:18-27). They know that the cost involved in being God's people is worth it. They have the sort of life that goes on forever in unequalled quality, rather than the transitory life that their peers are chasing.

(e) And The Cost Comes With An Overarching Comfort

For those of us who have decided to pay the cost of following Jesus, God promises an overarching comfort through this passage in Daniel. He undertakes to be with us.

He says he will remain firm to us as we remain firm to him. He will be with us in our deepest need and finally vindicate us as he vindicated his Son, Jesus. What is more, the time will come when he will show up all stupidity and foolishness for what it is, and reality and truth will triumph.

If we are Christians, we stand in direct line with Shadrach, Meshach, Abednego, Daniel, Jesus, Stephen, Paul, and countless others throughout the ages who have chosen to follow God. As we stand in line we must realise that at sometime in our life their stand must be our stand and their words our words. For some of us it will be in the office, workplace, amongst student friends, and the like. Here the cost may be our reputation, friendships, promotions, jobs and livelihood. For some Christians the cost has been or will be made in the face of live persecutors with instruments of death and torture. Here the cost will be pain, disfigurement and perhaps even death. Reality always comes with a price. No matter which it is for us, should God call upon us to suffer for being his, he will stand with us as he did with each of these. He will walk with us in the midst of the fire as he did with Shadrach, Meshach and Abednego.

FOR STUDY, DISCUSSION AND PRAYER

1. In what areas are Christians in our community most exposed to the danger of compromising their faith? In what areas are you most vulnerable to the danger of compromising your faith?

2. Read 1 Corinthians 10:1-11:1. Put the message of the chapter into your own words (no more than three sentences). What does 1 Corinthians 10:13 mean within this larger context? What importance does it have for us as we face temptation?

11

No Longer Human
4:1-37

1. The Epistle of Nebuchadnezzar

(a) A Story Worth Hearing

This chapter is unusual in the first six chapters of the book
of Daniel. It is not only cast in direct speech, but the direct
speech of Nebuchadnezzar. We have other examples of first
person narration (for example, Nehemiah's memoirs,
Ecclesiastes, the latter chapters of Daniel). Nevertheless,
Daniel 4 is unique in that it is the only example of it being
used in a short story, and on the lips of someone outside the
family of Israel.

Furthermore, Daniel 4 is cast in the form of a royal
encyclical or epistle, with an opening identification of the
writer and those he is addressing, and a greeting: *'I,
Nebuchadnezzar, To all peoples, nations and men of every
language, who live in all the world: May you prosper greatly.'* This
form gives it a strong feeling of reality and authority. What
was related was important and of great personal significance
to its author, Nebuchadnezzar.

The use of direct speech and the universal address (that is,
*peoples, nations and men of every language, who live in all the
world*) also draws us, and other readers, into the narrative in

a way that chapters 1-3 had not. We are being addressed personally. This epistle is not only for the subjects of Nebuchadnezzar in a particular time and place, but for us as well. The things said in it are not only important for Nebuchadnezzar. They are also important for us.

Nebuchadnezzar pressed on. He told the conclusion of his story before telling its beginning. *The Most High God* had performed some *signs and wonders* in his life that had resulted in his being able to say about him the sorts of things Israelites said about him in their psalms of praise.

> *How great are his signs, how mighty his wonders! His kingdom is an eternal kingdom; his dominion endures from generation to generation.*

This was a story that was so significant for Nebuchadnezzar that it caused him to write a public document to a wide audience and to praise the God of a nation whose God he had defeated and whose temple vessels he had locked up in temples of his own gods. This was a story worth listening to.

(b) Signs And Wonders

The term 'signs and wonders' occurs less than twenty times in the Old Testament. It was generally used to speak of God's great action in redeeming his people from Egypt (Exodus 7:3; Deuteronomy 4:34; 6:22; 7:19; 26:8; 34:11; Nehemiah 9:10; Psalm 135:9; Jeremiah 32:20). This great event was the occasion for God showing himself and his might and power to both the Israelites and the nation of Egypt. It was the demonstration that he was indeed God.

When Nebuchadnezzar used the term here the effect was to liken the experience he related in this chapter to that of the Exodus for Jews. It was an act in which God made known to him his sovereignty and power. It was an act in which God 'gained renown' (cf Jeremiah 32:20).

Again, this claim by Nebuchadnezzar would have the effect of drawing any Jewish reader deeper into the story. How could this man, who conquered Jerusalem (chapter 1), who was due for destruction as the head of a human kingdom set against God (chapter 2), and who was a well-known idolater and persecutor of God's people, come to say such great things about God? This was a story worth hearing!

2. The Story

(a) A Dream Which Troubled And Terrified (4:4-9)

These days had been good ones for Nebuchadnezzar. His kingdom was secure and the warring was at a lull. Most of his building projects were completed (cf 4:30) and he was at peace in all ways, *contented and prosperous*. He had felt himself to be at a stage where he could enjoy the kingdom which he had created. He was a self-made man in a self-made world.

His peace was shattered by *a dream*. Each night it was repeated. *Lying in bed*, horrifying *images* and frightening *visions . . . passed through* his *mind*. He awoke *terrified*, disturbed and haunted. As with the previous dream (Daniel 2), he sought interpreters and *all the wise men of Babylon*. As before, he *commanded* that they *be brought before* him *to interpret the dream*. However, this time he did not threaten the *magicians, enchanters, astrologers and diviners* with rewards and punishments nor did he refuse to tell them the dream. Nevertheless, again they could not interpret it and failed to perform, despite their dream manuals and divination. Finally Daniel came into the king's presence and he told him the dream.

At this point Nebuchadnezzar noted that this Daniel was the same one who was *called Belteshazzar after the name of my god* (cf Daniel 1:6) and in whom there is *the spirit of the holy gods* (Daniel 2:11, 46-47). By this stage Daniel was obviously recognised by Nebuchadnezzar as a man with a curious mixture of the human and divine, a wise man with a remarkable ability to solve mysteries and interpret dreams. It was with such confidence that Nebuchadnezzar put the problem to him:

> *'Belteshazzar, chief of the magicians, I know that the spirit of the holy gods is in you, and no mystery is too difficult for you. Here is my dream; interpret it for me.'*

(b) The Content Of The Dream (4:10-18)

The dream was certainly graphic. It was of a great tree reaching into heaven, visible to the whole world because of its enormity. *Its leaves were beautiful and its fruit abundant.* It could have fed anything or anyone who came to it. It provided shelter and sustenance for all the field and birds of the air.

A heavenly messenger then burst in and ordered the lopping of the tree. It was cut down to a stump, its branches trimmed, leaves stripped off and fruit scattered. All the animals and birds which had been sheltered by it and flourished on its fruit fled from under it and from its branches. Finally the leftover stump was *bound with iron and bronze*, leaving a pitiful *stump* standing as a dismal reminder of its once glorious majesty.

According to the dream the one represented by the tree was then given over to the forces of nature to share the lot of a brute beast. He grovelled with the animals and plants in the dust of the earth with a mind that was little better than that of the beasts with which he shared his food.

The dream finished with another angelic announcement that the duration of this state would be *seven times* and that the purpose of the events depicted would be that the living might *know that the Most High is sovereign over the kingdoms of men*. It was so that they might wake up to the fact that he gave his authority to *anyone he wishes*, even to *the lowliest of men*.

There are various puzzling aspects of the dream. We are not told the identity of the messenger except that he seemed to be supernatural (*a holy one, coming down from heaven*). On the other hand, we are told that the purpose of the dream was that communication be made known to *the living* (that is, the dreamer, Nebuchadnezzar).

The image of a tree is a familiar one in the Bible, although it is used in a two-fold manner. In some passages it refers to the house of David, the Messiah and therefore to salvation (cf Isaiah 11:1-3, 10; Ezekiel 17:22-24; Hosea 14:5-7). In others it is an image of judgment, especially as exercised against political powers who have exalted themselves and overstepped their God-appointed role and the boundaries set for them by him (cf Isaiah 2:13; 10:33-34; Ezekiel 31:3-12). This two-fold nature is seen in this dream. The tree was *beautiful, its fruit abundant, and on it was food for all*. However, at the same time it reached up to the sky, asserting itself against God and promising to supply all the needs of all people. As such it was idolatrous and was therefore under divine condemnation, needing to be cut down, trimmed, and stripped of its leaves and fruit.

Having announced the content of the dream, Nebuchadnezzar reiterated his request:

> '*Now, Belteshazzar, tell me what it means, for none of the wise men in my kingdom can interpret it for me. But you can, because the spirit of the holy gods is in you.* '

(c) The Interpretation Of The Dream (4:19-27)

The more Daniel thought about the dream the more it *perplexed* him and *his thoughts terrified him*. There was no doubt that the dream was not good news for the king and did not speak well for him or for his future. However, the king was curious and kept pressing Daniel, assuring him that neither *the dream nor its meaning* should *alarm* him.

Daniel warned Nebuchadnezzar, saying: *'My lord, if only the dream applied to your enemies and its meaning to your adversaries!'* He then went on to interpret the dream. His interpretation was as follows:

> *'The tree you saw, which grew large and strong, with its top touching the sky, visible to the whole earth, with beautiful leaves and abundant fruit, providing food for all, giving shelter to the beasts of the field, and having nesting places in its branches for the birds of the air – you, O king, are that tree! You have become great and strong; your greatness has grown until it reaches the sky, and your dominion extends to distant parts of the earth.*

> *You, O king, saw a messenger, a holy one, coming down from heaven and saying, 'Cut down the tree and destroy it, but leave the stump, bound with iron and bronze, in the grass of the field, while its roots remain in the ground. Let him be drenched with the dew of heaven; let him live like the wild animals, until seven times pass by for him.'*

> *This is the interpretation, O king, and this is the decree the Most High has issued against my lord the king: You will be driven away from people and will live with the wild animals; you will eat grass like cattle and be drenched with the dew of heaven. Seven times will pass by for you until you acknowledge that the Most High is sovereign over the kingdoms of men and gives them to anyone he wishes. The command to leave the stump of the tree*

*with its roots means that your kingdom will be restored to you
when you acknowledge that Heaven rules.'*

The main points of the interpretation are straightforward:

- The dream was about Nebuchadnezzar. He was the tree of the dream. He was the one who had become great and strong, whose greatness had grown to reach the sky itself. His dominion stretched out to the distant parts of the earth. Nations nestled in his branches and had found security in his rule.

- He was the one who would be cut down until only a stump remained. He was to be the one who would be stricken with madness and driven out to live with wild beasts and eat grass like an ox for seven long years. He was the great king who would wake up every morning with the mind of an animal and find himself drenched with dew from sleeping out in the open.

- The purpose of this experience would be that he acknowledged that his sovereignty was a derived sovereignty, not an autonomous one. It was given by a Most High God who gave authority to whomever he wished.

- The command to leave the stump with its roots still in the ground was an indication that the kingdom would be restored and renewed with the recognition and confession that God was the sole sovereign. At this point he would wake up and his reason would be restored. The dream was not a message of utter destruction.

Daniel's obligation was to deliver the message from God. Perhaps he knew and suspected that Nebuchadnezzar would not do much in response, however, his obligation was not to force a response but to declare God's word and to advise and challenge as God directed. This he did in verse 27.

'Therefore, O king, be pleased to accept my advice: Renounce your sins by doing what is right, and your wickedness by being kind to the oppressed. It may be that then your prosperity will continue.'

In the Old Testament the kingship of God is generous, forgiving, merciful and overflowing with justice and righteousness. Israelite kings were urged to exercise the rule of God by ruling like him, by judging people in righteousness and the oppressed with justice (cf Psalm 72). They were required to live by the law of God and act like him (Deuteronomy 17:14-20; Ezekiel 34:1-6). Nebuchadnezzar was under the same obligations. His rule was a delegated rule and was not to be used for domination and subjugation but for serving the needs of those who were ruled. Daniel appeared to be aware that if Nebuchadnezzar was to realise the delegated nature of his kingship and submit to the demand by God to rule rightly and kindly then there would be no need for judgment and the peace and prosperity he had felt until now would continue unabated. As it was, he refused.

(d) The Dream Fulfilled (4:28-33)

Within *twelve months* the prophecy was fulfilled. One day, *as the king was walking on the roof of the royal palace of Babylon*, surveying his handiwork and soaking up the greatness of his achievements, he murmured to himself, *'Is not this the great Babylon I have built as the royal residence, by my mighty power and for the glory of my majesty.'*

The situation in which Nebuchadnezzar said these words was important. The roof of an ancient near eastern palace was usually a high roof, above the rest of the buildings in the city, except perhaps the temple. This showed the importance of the king. It also allowed him a vantage point from which to survey his own greatness and ponder his own achievements. For this reason, walking on a palace roof was often associated with security and pride. It was from a palace roof that David saw Bathsheba in 2 Samuel 11. Perhaps, like Nebuchadnezzar he was in a frame of mind which said, 'I have fought hard for all of this. It is mine, all mine.' Palace rooves were places of pride and therefore places of danger for kings who were given their rule by God and who were supposed to exercise it under the rule of God.

The words themselves are telling ones. With their mention of *I have built . . .by my mighty power . . . for the glory of my majesty*, there was no recognition of God or ascription of greatness to him. There was no acknowledgment that the rule, prosperity and peace he experienced was a gift from God. On the contrary, Nebuchadnezzar's words were full of 'I' and 'my.' They were still on his lips when the voice came from heaven.

> *'This is what is decreed for you, King Nebuchadnezzar. Your royal authority has been taken away from you. You will be driven away from people and will live with the wild animals; you will eat grass like cattle. Seven times will pass by for you until you acknowledge that the Most High is sovereign over the kingdoms of men and gives them to anyone he wishes.'*

Madness came just as it had been foreseen. Nebuchadnezzar was driven out to live with wild animals. *He was driven away from people and ate grass like cattle. His body was drenched with the dew of heaven until his hair grew as long as the feathers of an eagle and his nails like the claws of a bird.* He *ate grass like cattle* and woke every morning to find himself *drenched with the dew of heaven.* He had acted and behaved like an animal rather than a man living in the image of God, ruling the world under God's rule. As a result he found himself in an animal's place, having no human dignity and no human reason.

(e) Nebuchadnezzar Restored (4:34-37)

For seven long years he lived in this state before things changed. After seven years he *raised* his *eyes toward heaven*, symbolically repenting of his pride, with the result that his *sanity was restored*. Finally he acknowledged the sovereignty of heaven and recognised that the Most High was the ruler of all rulers. Where he had honoured himself previously, he now honoured and glorified our God, saying. . .

> *His dominion is an eternal dominion; his kingdom endures from generation to generation. All the peoples of the earth are regarded as nothing. He does as he pleases with the powers of heaven and the peoples of the earth. No one can hold back his hand or say to him: 'What have you done?'*

Again, the word usage is important. Where Nebuchadnezzar had stressed *I have built . . . by my mighty power . . . for the glory of my majesty*, he now recognises that *his kingdom endures . . . He does as he pleases . . . No one can hold back his hand*.

God acted with characteristic mercy when Nebuchadnezzar repented. Not only was Nebuchadnezzar's *sanity restored*, but also his *kingdom* was restored and regained its *glory and splendour*, his *advisers and nobles* rallied around him yet again, and he extolled the King of heaven who *does as he pleases with the powers of heaven and the peoples of the earth*. Such a God as this does what *is right* and *just* and is *able to humble . . . those who walk in pride*.

However, before we become too enthusiastic about Nebuchadnezzar's confession and acknowledgment of God's sovereignty, we should again take a close look at his use of words. Although he moves from 'I' and 'my' to 'him', 'he' and 'his', the transition is not at all complete. At the close of the chapter he is back to talking in terms of *my honour and splendour . . . my kingdom . . . my advisers and nobles . . . my throne.* Nebuchadnezzar's praise of God in these final verses was matched by his praise of himself. Nebuchadnezzar was still fickle and his repentance far from complete.

3. What Is The Point?

The point of the story appears to be that God is the true king of the world, that he delegates his kingship to human beings in history and that he has certain expectations as to how that kingship should be practised by them. This account, and the one that follows in Daniel 5, tell us that when confronted with such an obligation, human beings react in a variety of ways at a variety of times. Those who rule well are those who

- humble themselves;
- acknowledge the overarching rule of God; and
- treat God's things and people with respect.

Rulers must do what Nebuchadnezzar finally did. They must recognise God's overarching sovereignty and rule and that all rule derives from him. This is to see things reasonably. This perspective is the one which puts life and human rule in its proper place.

FOR STUDY, DISCUSSION AND PRAYER

1. In what sense were the events which happened to Nebuchadnezzar in this chapter and to Daniel in his rescue in chapter 6, 'signs and wonders' according to the usual Biblical use of this phrase?

2. Read through the interpretation of Nebuchadnezzar's dream given by Daniel. What are his main points?

3. Read Deuteronomy 17:14-20, Psalm 72, Ezekiel 34:1-6 and 1 Peter 5:1-4. According to these passages, what are the marks of true godly leadership?

4. Think about the relationships you are in where you are in authority over others. Is the authority which you exercise similar to that which is portrayed in the passages in Question 3? Spend time repenting of any misuse of your authority and praying about your future use of it.

12

The Writing is On The Wall 5:1-31

1. The Other Side Of The Coin

As we noted in the introduction, chapters 4 and 5 belong together. They both concern the interaction between God as king and a human king. Chapter 5 complements the previous chapter. It gives us a picture of a king who was proud and who shook his fist at God. He had no room for repentance and acknowledgment of God.

(a) The Last Days of Belshazzar

(i) Who was Belshazzar?

The Belshazzar mentioned here was probably the same Belshazzar mentioned in Neo-Babylonian tablets. These tablets refer to Nabonidus as the final king of the Babylonian Empire and associate his eldest son, Belshazzar, with him on an equal footing. Because of frequent and long campaigns by Nabonidus in Arabia, Belshazzar acted as regent in Babylon.

(ii) The Banquet Of Belshazzar (5:1-4)

There is evidence within the chapter that Belshazzar was in a precarious position, needing to bolster his kingdom and his right to be seen as king. He was not king in his own right. Unlike Nebuchadnezzar, he had not earned it and so needed to buy respect and support with food, wine and entertainment. Perhaps it was this that caused *King Belshazzar* to give *a great banquet for a thousand of his nobles* and to drink *wine with them.*

Perhaps such a feast also provided opportunity to do something quite extraordinary and provocative. He took something of Nebuchadnezzar's, something he had considered sacred, *the gold and silver goblets that Nebuchadnezzar his father had taken from the temple in Jerusalem,* and drank from them. However, they were vessels *from the temple of God in Jerusalem.* In other words, Belshazzar perhaps had taken the vessels because they represented Nebuchadnezzar and his achievements, but in doing so he had engaged in a conflict with the God from whose temple they came. He had taken something his father treated as sacred and refused to treat it in the same way. It was an act of defiance towards Nebuchadnezzar. However, it was also an act of defiance against the God of Israel.

The vessels were retrieved and distributed among the guests so that *the king and his nobles, his wives and his concubines drank from them.* As they did the defiance against the God of Israel escalated, for *they praised the gods of gold and silver, of bronze and iron, wood and stone.*

By acting as he did, albeit innocently and probably under the influence of a little too much alcohol, Belshazzar was throwing down the gauntlet to the God from whose temple they were taken. He was attempting to bring God under his control and subject to his ridicule.

As Daniel would later remind Belshazzar, he was acting in a way Nebuchadnezzar had learnt to renounce, asserting himself against God in a way Nebuchadnezzar had replaced with recognition, honour and praise.

(iii) God's Graffiti (5:5-9)

God responded to the defiance of Belshazzar. While the gods of gold, silver, bronze, iron, wood and stone remained mute, a disembodied hand and fingers *appeared and wrote on the plaster of the wall, near the lampstand in the royal palace.* The king watched *the hand as it wrote* and then, as he panicked, *his face turned pale* and he became so frightened that *his knees knocked together and his legs gave way. He called out for his enchanters, astrologers and diviners*, commanding them and offering them bribes. He begged them to discern the graffiti on the wall. It was no use, not only did the gods of gold, silver, bronze, iron, wood and stone remain mute, their representatives also remained mute.

(iv) Someone Who Could Interpret (5:10-17)

The result was that *King Belshazzar became more and more terrified and his face grew more pale.* He knew that what had happened was divine in origin and needed an interpretation. Eventually *the queen, hearing the voices of the king and his nobles*, came to the rescue and said:

'Don't be alarmed! Don't look so pale! There is a man in your kingdom who has the spirit of the holy gods in him. In the time of your father he was found to have insight and intelligence and wisdom like that of the gods. King Nebuchadnezzar your father – your father the king, I say – appointed him chief of the magicians, enchanters, astrologers and diviners. This man Daniel, whom the king called Belteshazzar, was found to have a keen mind and knowledge and understanding, and also the ability to interpret

dreams, explain riddles and solve difficult problems. Call for Daniel, and he will tell you what the writing means.'

Again Daniel was called in and the king reiterated the words of the queen (probably a reference to the queen mother). He offered huge incentives to Daniel to read this writing and tell the king what it meant. The incentives were the *purple* of royalty, *a gold chain* and the *third highest* position in the kingdom.

(v) Two Kinds of Kings (5:18-24)

(A) Good King Nebuchadnezzar

Daniel rejected the gifts but agreed to *read the writing for the king* and tell him what it meant. Before long the meaning became evident. It was related to the incident with Nebuchadnezzar. Daniel refreshed his memory before delivering the prophecy and the threat evident in the writing on the wall.

> *'O king, the Most High God gave your father Nebuchadnezzar sovereignty and greatness and glory and splendour. Because of the high position he gave him, all the peoples and nations and men of every language dreaded and feared him. Those the king wanted to put to death, he put to death; those he wanted to spare, he spared; those he wanted to promote, he promoted; and those he wanted to humble, he humbled. But when his heart became arrogant and hardened with pride, he was deposed from his royal throne and stripped of his glory. He was driven away from people and given the mind of an animal; he lived with the wild donkeys and ate grass like cattle; and his body was drenched with the dew of heaven, until he acknowledged that the Most High God is sovereign over the kingdoms of men and sets over them anyone he wishes.'*

The tone of the words was prophetic and the thrust was clear: Even though the rule of Nebuchadnezzar had been grand, Nebuchadnezzar had learnt that his rule was a given rule, deriving from a greater ruler, God.

(B) Not So Good Belshazzar

Having rehearsed Nebuchadnezzar's history in a positive light, Daniel immediately drew the contrast with the words *but you his son, O Belshazzar*. The contrast was marked: Belshazzar had not learnt from his father. *Though* he *knew all this* he had *not humbled* himself before the ruler of the whole earth, *the Lord of heaven*, but had flagrantly thrown down the gauntlet to him and challenged him to a duel. He had lifted himself up against the Lord of heaven by drinking from this real God's sacred vessels while praising *gods of gold, silver, bronze, iron, wood and stone*. There was no recognition that all he was and all he had was a gift from the true God. He did not *honour the God who* held *in his hand* his life and all his *ways*. For this reason God had acted by sending a message to Belshazzar. The message contained a threat to him, a self-made, blasphemous man.

(vi) The Message (5:25-28)

The message was short and to the point . . .MENE, MENE, TEKEL, PARSIN. The words describe coinage.

MENA	=	a mena
TEKEL	=	Aramaic spelling of 'shekel'
PARSIN	=	a half mena

The relation among the three was 60:1:30. A modern equivalent would be a hand on the wall writing something like, 'A dollar, a dollar, two cents, fifty cents.' It was cryptic and therefore it was no wonder that the Chaldeans could not interpret it. However, God gave the interpretation to Daniel. Each of the words was a pun.

MENE is related to the verb MNH, meaning 'numbered';

TEKEL is related to the verb TQL, meaning 'weighed';

and PARSIN is related to the verb PRS, meaning 'divided'.

The point was therefore:

- MENE – *God has numbered the days of your reign and brought it to an end.*

Belshazzar's destiny could not be changed. It was coming and could not be averted.

- TEKEL – *You have been weighed on the scales and found wanting.*

Belshazzar's rule had been weighed and found wanting. The importance of a kingdom is not measured by its size or by the weight of the centuries of history that it survives. It is weighed by its reason for being and Babylon under Belshazzar had been weighed in this manner and found deficient.

- PARSIN – *Your kingdom is divided and given to the Medes and the Persians.*

Belshazzar's kingdom would be divided. It would be divided into two. Half would go to the Medes and half to the Persians (the word for Persia also sounds like the verb PRS).

Having revealed God's judgment, Daniel was rewarded. However, it did not last long, for that night Belshazzar also received his reward. He was killed by a new king from a new nation. One great kingdom vanished and a new kingdom found its temporary place in history.

(vii) Darius the Mede

The reference to Darius the Mede in 5:30 is strange. Writers of the Bible (including Daniel, cf Daniel 1:21 and 5:28) were aware that it was Cyrus the Great of Persia who toppled Babylon. Moreover, there was no Darius on the throne until 522 BC.

Various proposals to solve this problem have been suggested. Although none of the solutions are without difficulty the most likely would appear to be the suggestion that Darius the Mede is the same person as Cyrus.

3. Nebuchadnezzar Versus Belshazzar

The contrast and point of comparison between chapter 4 and chapter 5 and the two principal characters within those chapters are evident. There were kings who ruled well and kings who ruled badly. Those who ruled badly were those who

- refused to humble themselves;
- did not acknowledge the overarching rule of God; and
- did not treat God's things and people with respect.

Belshazzar was one who ruled badly. Although he had history to warn him, he had not learnt. He defied the Lord of heaven and profaned what had been dedicated to him, worshipping lifeless gods while flaunting the rule of the real God. There was not even a momentary recognition from him to the God to whom he owed his very existence, let alone his kingship.

Belshazzar viewed himself and his rule as autonomous and independent. In his pride he wilfully suppressed the truth and his pride decided his fate. Destruction came swiftly.

God acted and another, a chosen one from God, was put in his place. For pride goes before destruction and a haughty spirit before a fall (Proverbs 16:18).

FOR STUDY, DISCUSSION AND PRAYER

1. In what way do rulers in our world 'shake their fist' at God?

2. Is the best ruler necessarily Christian? Why? Why not?

3. From chapters 4 and 5 of Daniel, what is it that God requires of those to whom he gives leadership and authority?

4. What comparisons are made between Nebuchadnezzar and Belshazzar within chapters 4 and 5?

5. Read 1 Timothy 2. What does Paul urge us to do for those in authority? Why? Spend some time praying as he suggests.

13

Understanding the Kingdom of God (II)

1. The Kingship of God

Once more it will be useful to summarise what we have discovered from our study of the book of Daniel. Last time we did this, in chapter 8, we established three building blocks in our understanding of the kingdom of God.

- As Creator of the world, God is its one true king.
- The kingship of God is headed toward a goal: the world living under God as king and the end of all rivals to his kingship.
- God delegates his kingship to human beings.

Each of the these points are either illustrated or can be inferred in chapters 4 and 5. For example, throughout both chapters we are told that God is King. He is the Most High God, the one sovereign over the world. Both chapters stress the need for human rulers to live under God as King and of his opposition to those who refuse to do so. Both chapters take up the idea that the kingship exercised by both Nebuchadnezzar and Belshazzar was delegated kingship.

(a) A Just and Merciful Ruler

There are some additional points about the kingship of God which we need to understand in order to grapple with the message of chapter 4. Readers of the Old Testament could not fail but be aware of the nature of God's kingship. They knew him to be a ruler who was not harsh or tyrannical but loving, full of justice, mercy and compassion. Psalm 145, a hymn celebrating the kingship of God, taught them that:

> The Lord is gracious and compassionate, slow to anger and rich in love. The Lord is good to all; he has compassion on all he has made. All you have made will praise you, O Lord; your saints will extol you. They will tell of the glory of your Kingdom and speak of your might, so that all men may know of your mighty acts and the glorious splendour of your Kingdom. Your Kingdom is an everlasting Kingdom, and your dominion endures throughout all generations.

> The Lord is faithful to his promises and loving towards all he has made. The Lord upholds all those who fall and lifts up all who are bowed down. The eyes of all look to you, and you give them their food at the proper time. You open your hand and satisfy the desires of every living thing. (Psalm 145:8-16)

The words applied to God are striking. He is a King who is *gracious* and *compassionate, slow to anger* and *rich in love.* He is *good* to all, *faithful* to his promises and *loving* towards all he has made, *upholding* all those who fall and *lifting up* all who are bowed down. He is generous to all the earth, *opening his hand, giving* and *satisfying* the desires of every living thing. God's kingly rule is characterised by justice, goodness, compassion, faithfulness, love and mercy. He is a creator who always has the best interests of his creation in mind.

It is this nature of God's kingship that gives us our next building block.

- God's kingly rule is characterised by justice and mercy.

The nature of God's kingly rule is not just intended to impact on his direct rule of creation. The Old Testament is clear that the method and nature of his rule is to be the pattern for human beings who rule under him. That is why kings of Israel were challenged to judge people in righteousness and treat the oppressed with justice (Psalm 72).

Endow the king with your justice, O God, the royal son with your righteousness. He will judge your people in righteousness, your afflicted ones with justice.

For he will deliver the needy who cry out, the afflicted who have no-one to help. He will take pity on the weak and the needy and save the needy from death. He will rescue them from oppression and violence, for precious is their blood in his sight. (Psalm 72:1-2, 12-14)

God gives his rule to people so that they might rule as he rules. It is not for the purpose of domination and subjugation but for serving the needs of those who are ruled. It is this truth that stood behind Daniel's advice to Nebuchadnezzar and which helps us understand it.

'Therefore, O king, be pleased to accept my advice: Renounce your sins by doing what is right, and your wickedness by being kind to the oppressed. It may be that then your prosperity will continue.'

(b) No Longer Human

In chapter 8 we learned that God delegates his rule. We can see some of what this means in chapter 4. In this chapter Nebuchadnezzar was again spoken of in terms reminiscent of Adam (Daniel 4:18 cf 2:37-38). He, a pagan king, was to exercise God's rule over God's world as God's representative as Adam was meant to have done. He was to rule with recognition of God's overarching rule and in imitation of that rule.

Therefore, when Nebuchadnezzar turned his back on God as sovereign and set himself up as sovereign, he was turning his back on his own humanity, on the image of God. This was what was happening when Nebuchadnezzar returned to an animal. He had turned his back on exercising the rule of God and acted autonomously. He was no longer acting as the image of God, as a human being should act. At this point he was no better than an animal.

(c) Recognising Delegated Rule

Because all rule is given and delegated, it is by nature subject to a higher authority. The stories in the book of Daniel have given prominence to this. All rule must be subject to the Most High, the God of heaven, and those who exercise it must think and act with him in mind. Rulers must acknowledge that the Most High is sovereign over the kingdoms of men and sets over them anyone he wishes. Rulers must be God-like in their rule, doing what is right and being kind to the oppressed.

This gives us our next building block

- Every human being must recognise that whatever rule he or she has is a gift of God, delegated to them by God.

(d) Reacting to the Rule of God

The story of Nebuchadnezzar in chapter 4 illustrates one of the two reactions to the rule of God. Although he took great pride in his achievement as king, he eventually learned, through his experience of living with the wild animals for seven years, to acknowledge the sovereignty of God. He confessed:

> *How great are his signs and mighty his wonders! His Kingdom is an eternal Kingdom; his dominion endures from generation to generation.*

The story of Belshazzar illustrates one side of the coin. Belshazzar possessed the world's crown as a gift from God and yet flaunted it. He perceived himself as autonomous and independent, able to challenge God's rule and defy him. History will be full of men and women like Belshazzar. Our world has been and will be full of kingdoms like his.

This leads to our next building block:

* The Kingdom of God is both a threat and a promise.

(i) The Kingdom of God as a threat

It is a threat to those who possess power in the human domain and cherish it as a thing to be used autonomously and independently. It is a threat to those who take the power delegated to them from God and use it in the interest of self. The story of Belshazzar speaks to people like this and tells them that human sovereignty is not autonomous but always subject to a greater power. It is always accountable.

This is not welcome news. Many of us have power and our own little kingdoms. So many of us have thrown ourselves into working for our own kingdom, for our own glory and have done so in open rebellion to the God who gives all rule and authority. To such people as Belshazzar and maybe even us, God promises that he will act. He will take authority from us, shattering and devastating us with his own sovereign rule.

To some of the rulers of the world this judgment will come soon, as it did with Belshazzar. To others it will come later. God cannot fail to act, and to think otherwise is to throw down the gauntlet to him and face certain defeat.

On the other side of the coin, the rule of God comes in a much more positive way. It comes as a promise for the future. It came in this way for those who were in exile in Babylon.

For them the rule of God would have been the long-term basis for their hope. It promised that there would be a future age where the just and the righteous will rule on behalf of the sovereign Lord, the Just One. The rule of God looks towards a time and place where the saints of the Most High will be given power and sovereignty as the only ones fit to rule like God. This is where history is headed. It is moving towards a goal of humans living as they were created to live as the image of God, ruling the world under the rule of God.

This is where Genesis 1 is heading. It is confirmed by the failure of Nebuchadnezzar and Belshazzar. There will be a day when there will be one who lives under the rule of God, who subjects his rule to the rule of God and rules in a God-like manner. There will be one who is as a brother (Deuteronomy 17:14-20), who has the best interests of others in mind, who gives up his rights for others and lives in justice, mercy and kindness.

(ii) The Kingdom of God as a promise

Others in the Old Testament had seen the promise inherent in the concept of the rule of God and had looked for an ideal ruler. Ezekiel saw him as a new Davidic leader, describing him as a shepherd who would care for his flock in contrast to the kings and leaders who had ruled Israel in the past. He would not be one who took advantage of those he ruled over, eating the curds, clothing himself with the wool, slaughtering the choice animals and not caring for the flock. His rule would not be harsh and brutal. Rather, he would be one who searched for the lost and brought back the strays. He would strengthen the weak and bind up the injured, tending them in good pasture and he would make them lie down in rest and security (see Ezekiel 34).

Isaiah saw this ideal ruler as a servant. He was one who would be despised and rejected, a man of sorrows and familiar with suffering. He would be a lowly figure who took the infirmity, sorrow, transgression and punishment of those whom he would lead. He would be one so God-like that he would act in a way totally devoid of self interest and totally consumed with the well-being of those over whom he would rule, (see Isaiah 52:13-53:12).

2. Looking For The Perfect Man

As we look back over the years we would concur with Daniel and the rest of the Old Testament. Human beings have never quite handled the kingship of God appropriately. Our nature is like that of our forefather, Adam, in snatching after being like God. We are all the same. Our nature is to do things our own way without God, to take upon ourselves the credentials of godhead.

However, while looking at the past and the present and acknowledging our dismal failure to improve the situation, we can add to Daniel's list of characteristics concerning the kingship of God:

- There is only one human being who has exercised the rule of God perfectly, Jesus. He is given the rule of God for all time.

As those who live after the coming of Christ we know that there is one human being who refused to act independently and autonomously. He humbled himself and obeyed, ruling in a God-like fashion by coming not to be served, but to serve and give his life as a ransom for many (Mark 10:45). He did what Adam never did, he emptied himself, not seeking to be equal with God, but took on the form of a servant (cf Philippians 2:1-12).

While we do not see any other human being acting in the image of God by ruling as a brother, seeking the best interests of others, we did see Jesus in this role. We saw one made a little lower than the angels, crowned with glory and honour because he suffered death, so that by the grace of God he might taste death for everyone (cf Hebrews 2:5-13). This was one made and who acted in the image of God, ruling under the rule of God, doing right and being kind to the oppressed. Here was man behaving as he was designed to do. He was humble, meek, obedient and exercising rule as it should be exercised, that is as delegated, God-given rule. Here is the sort of ruler before whom we can bow, which is why God highly exalted him and bestowed on him the name that is above every name, that at his name every knee should bow and every tongue confess that Jesus Christ is Lord to the glory of God the Father.

FOR STUDY, DISCUSSION AND PRAYER

1. What will 'authority exercised under the kingship of God' look like in practice?

2. In what sense does the ruler of God hold out hope for people?

3. Read Psalm 2, a psalm about God's rule through his Messiah. How is the idea of God's kingship as both threat and promise presented in the Psalm? What do we need to do in order to ensure that we are recipients of the promise rather than the threat?

4. Read Isaiah 52:13-53:12. What words and descriptions are used to describe an ideal ruler?

5. Read Mark 10:25-45. What is the difference between Jesus' view of authority and that of his disciples?

14

Choosing Your Allegiances
6:1-10

1. Putting Things Into Perspective

Daniel was not exempted from facing opposition for being God's person. Although he had to face opposition many times each day in small ways, there came a day when he too, like his friends Shadrach, Meshach and Abednego, faced it in an extraordinary way. He too became a victim of living in a world opposed to God and set against the people of God.

The story recorded in Daniel 6 is very similar to that recorded in Daniel 3 and in many ways parallels it. For this reason, it is helpful to remember some of the points which lay behind that story. First, Jews were different from the nations around them, a conspicuous and 'peculiar' people, intense and scrupulous about keeping the law of God.

Second, they were especially zealous about the commandments concerning allegiance to the one God alone and opposition to idolatry because it was these commandments which had brought them into exile.

Third being a loyal Jew in the king's court made a person visible and vulnerable and ready prey for anyone who was jealous of the position.

Fourth, the kings that Daniel served were kings who were only too well aware of the fragility of their kingdoms. They were continually facing problems maintaining their places and were therefore often fickle and manipulative in their day-to-day dealings with those who staffed their courts.

The Daniel we have met so far was no different to his friends. He also had their rock-like determination. Like them and the great ones before them, he was determined to keep his loyalty to God. He was determined to be loyal to God and therefore loyal to his law. Although loyalty to God was expressed differently in different times, he knew that in his case it would include loyalty to the law of God made clear through Moses. He was very vulnerable.

(a) The Story Of Joseph

However, the story of Daniel also bears striking resemblance to the circumstances and career of Joseph. Joseph ended up in a foreign land, serving as a high ranking official at the court of a pagan king. He was skilled in the interpretation of dreams and learned in the language and ways of the nation he served. He had been tempted to break loyalty with the God of his fathers by engaging in adultery (Genesis 39) but had refused and faced the consequences of his refusal. He had also experienced, like Shadrach, Meshach and Abednego, divine deliverance. (Although not quite as immediately as they had done. He had rotted in a prison for some time waiting for it!).

Joseph displayed great skill whilst in Egypt, excelling in wisdom, surpassing his peers and pagan counterparts. He remained faithful to God, displaying moral integrity, courage, and the fear of God.

Perhaps in the story and experience of Joseph, Daniel found a pattern for God's dealing with people and the response he desired from them. Finding himself in Joseph's position, he acted like Joseph. He maintained his total allegiance to the God of his fathers while not rejecting the good things which did not run contrary to scriptural faith. At the same time he would have learnt a pattern of God's activity from Joseph, noting that God chooses such people as Joseph to be part of his larger purposes. God remains faithful to those who remain faithful to him, vindicating and blessing those who choose the path of loyalty rather than compromise.

For someone who knew the story of Joseph, the experiences of Shadrach, Meshach and Abednego came as no surprise. They confirmed the character of God already known from the Scriptures.

2. A New Order

In the early days of his reign Darius the Mede made moves to decentralise his government by appointing *120 satraps to rule throughout the kingdom, with three administrators over them, one of whom was Daniel. Now Daniel so distinguished himself among the administrators and the satraps by his exceptional qualities that the king planned to set him over the whole kingdom.*

3. Closing the Trap

(a) ... On Daniel

The inevitable day came. People seeing Daniel's exceptional ability and his loyalty to the king and his devotion to the things of his God seized the opportunity. As Daniel became more prominent and the king moved to promote him even further there was no shortage of jealousy amongst the other court officials. They started to plan his demise by trying *to find grounds for charges* against him *in his conduct of government affairs, but they were unable to do so.*

It was understandable that Daniel had risen to such prominence. He was the sort of person on whom rulers depend. There was *no corruption in him, because he was trustworthy and neither corrupt nor negligent.* He was a model of the godly person at work. It is a model we see picked up in the New Testament in a variety of places. He worked with all his heart as though he was working for the Lord, not just a human master (cf Ephesians 6:5-8; Colossians 3:22-25; 1 Peter 2:13-25).

Having found no fault with his public life and no possibility of doing so, *these men* pried into his private life (a familiar ploy, used in political life even in our own day!). They realised that they would not be able to trap him *unless it* had *something to do with the law of his God.* They therefore decided to play off his loyalty to the king against his devotion to his God. The contest would take place through pitting the law of the Medes and the Persians against the law of God. They had no doubt which choice Daniel would make. They knew his devotion to his God far exceeded his loyalty to any earthly king.

Their planning issued in a scheme which they were sure would work because it bargained on the king's arrogance and took advantage of his desire to unite his kingdom. It would defeat Daniel because it sandwiched him between two laws: the law of the Medes and the Persians and the law of God. There was no doubt as to which law he would choose.

The court officials therefore put the proposal before the king: *'O King Darius, live for ever! The royal administrators, prefects, satraps, advisers and governors have all agreed that the king should issue an edict and enforce the decree that anyone who prays to any god or man during the next thirty days, except to you, O king, shall be thrown into the lions' den. Now, O king, issue the decree and put it in writing so that it cannot be altered – in accordance with the laws of the Medes and Persians, which cannot be repealed.'*

There are a number of things to notice about this speech. The first is that it was a lie. Not all agreed to it. Daniel was the obvious exception. The second is that its intention, which lay under the surface and was not expressed, to trap Daniel, would probably never have been agreed to if it had been openly stated. On it's surface the proposal was good in that it bound the newly established kingdom together. This was a good move, especially in the light of decentralisation. However, underneath it actually did the reverse of what it proposed. It took away the king's freedom and allowed him to be manipulated by conspirators.

However, as expected, the king succumbed. The edict was written down and put into force. All that was needed was the evidence to convict Daniel. It was not long in coming, for when Daniel *learned that the decree had been published* he proceeded to go about his daily routine. At the same time as normal he went *to his upstairs room* and in the same way as usual he walked over to the *windows* of the room which faced *toward Jerusalem.* As he had always done, *three times a day*, he knelt *on his knees,* facing the ruins of Jerusalem, and prayed. As was his custom, he gave thanks to his God for all his mercy and kindness. He praised God for his grace in the present and for the future promise of salvation which would one day come to Jerusalem and all who looked towards its God.

Daniel did the predictable. As he had done when he first arrived and many times since, he engaged in civil disobedience. As his friends did before him, he broke the law, three times a day, by continuing his usual practice. He had no choice, but in so doing he sealed his downfall.

The reasons for Daniel's continued prayer and practice of praying toward Jerusalem were multiple but the primary reason probably had to do with the place of Babylon and Jerusalem in the purposes of his God.

(b) The Tale of Two cities

(i) Babylon

Magnificent though it was, Babylon and the concept behind it was not new. Babel, Babylon, Babylonia, the land of Shinar, all stood for the same thing. Each of these names symbolised human beings acting independently of God as they had at the Tower of Babel in Genesis 11, when they banded together and built a tower that reached to the heavens, making a name for themselves.

Daniel knew Babylon and he knew the character of Babylon. He knew that the name fitted well. The Babylon he lived in was no different from the Tower of Babel standing in the land of Shinar. It was a proud, autonomous city reaching up to the heavens in defiance of God and his rule. It was a city that had no fear of the real God and it represented a society which was proud of itself and confident in its own strategies, structures and strength.

Daniel also knew the fate of Babylon. As a human kingdom it would end in the dust. Genesis 11 and the prophets were clear. The fate of Babylon was beyond doubt. Had not Isaiah said 'disaster will come upon you' (Isaiah 14:12-15; 47:8-11) and Jeremiah warned that God 'will pay her what she deserves' (Jeremiah 51:6-9). Daniel knew with all the true prophets of God that our world is strewn with Babylons because Babylon was the kind of society which human beings build. Daniel therefore knew that the fate of human society as a man-built entity was the fierce fire of God's judgment.

(ii) Jerusalem

On the other hand, Jerusalem represented a different idea. Jerusalem was the city built by God, which came into existence because the Lord God said, 'She shall be inhabited.' She was the visible symbol of the presence, goodness, and purposefulness of God.

Daniel was committed to the plan and purpose of God, aware that it would not fail but would be accomplished. For him and many others, the city Jerusalem symbolised this because it was the city where God had fulfilled his promises and where he had demonstrated time and time again that he was God. Therefore to view Jerusalem was to view God himself. To walk around Jerusalem and look at it was to look to God himself.

> Walk about Zion, go round her, count her towers, consider well her ramparts, view her citadels, that you may tell of them to the next generation. For this is our God for ever and ever; he will be our guide even to the end. (Psalm 48:12-14)

Jerusalem was where reality was found, symbolising all that God had been and would be. It epitomised the desire of the nations, that is, the people of God living as friends with God under the rule of God in the place of God's choice.

Daniel also understood the teaching of Scriptures about the future of Jerusalem. As he knew the prophets' pronouncements concerning Babylon, he knew them concerning Jerusalem. Although Jerusalem had become a pile of rubble, he trusted God to be true to his promise that there would be a day when 'the moon will be abashed, the sun ashamed; for the Lord Almighty will reign on Mount Zion and in Jerusalem, and before its elders, gloriously' (Isaiah 24:23). If Babylon was a city doomed for destruction, Jerusalem was a city destined for salvation. Again, Isaiah had said that:

in the last days the mountain of the Lord's temple will be established as chief among the mountains; it will be raised above the hills, and all nations will stream to it. Many peoples will come and say, 'Come, let us go up to the mountain of the Lord, to the house of the God of Jacob. He will teach us of his ways, so that we may walk in his paths.' The law will go out from Zion, the word of the Lord from Jerusalem. (Isaiah 2:2-3; cf 25:6-9; 26:1-2)

All who were well versed in the Scriptures, as Daniel undoubtedly was, knew where their eyes must be set. Their focus must not be on Babylon nor on destruction. Their eyes must be fixed on the future, on Jerusalem. Regularly they sang the song of the exile:

By the rivers of Babylon we sat down and wept when we remembered Zion. There on the poplars we hung our harps, for there our captors asked of us songs, our tormentors demanded songs of joy; they said, 'Sing us one of the songs of Zion!'

How can we sing the songs of the Lord while in a foreign land? If I forget you, O Jerusalem, may my right hand forget its skill. May my tongue cling to the roof of my mouth if I do not remember you, if I do not consider Jerusalem my highest joy. (Psalm 137:5-6)

So when Daniel went and prayed *toward Jerusalem* he was not just facing a city because of some sentimental attachment to a pile of rubble that once represented a powerful nation. He was facing it and praying towards it because it was the city of God, the city from which God would one day send his deliverer. Neglecting to turn to Jerusalem was to neglect the future, to quench your vision, kill your spirit, and destroy your soul. Daniel could do no other. Jerusalem gave him his very reason for existence and he refused to hide it, no matter what the cost.

(c) Jesus And The Two Cities

(i) Babylon

The New Testament picks up this idea of two cities in the book of Revelation. Babylon, as the symbol of humanism – human existence with humanity at its centre – stands under the condemnation of God. Such existence runs against God's goal for his world and therefore cannot stand up against God's alternative, Jerusalem. It is doomed. For this reason the Bible ends with these words about it:

> Woe! Woe, O great city, O Babylon, city of power! In one hour your doom has come!

> Rejoice over her, O heaven! Rejoice, saints and apostles and prophets! God has judged her for the way she treated you.

> Then a mighty angel picked up a boulder the size of a large millstone and threw it into the sea, and said: 'With such violence the great city of Babylon will be thrown down, never to be found again.' (Revelation 18:10, 19-21)

(ii) Jerusalem

Jerusalem is also a biblical symbol. It stands for human existence with God at its centre and God in control. The Bible says that such human existence is God's goal for humanity and all that line themselves up with this goal will survive. Hence the Bible ends with these words about Jerusalem:

Then I saw a new heaven and a new earth, for the first heaven and the first earth had passed away, and there was no longer any sea. I saw the Holy City, the new Jerusalem, coming down out of heaven from God, prepared as a bride beautifully dressed for her husband. And I heard a loud voice from the throne saying, 'Now the dwelling of God is with men, and he will live with them. They will be his people, and God himself will be with them and be their God. He will wipe every tear from their eyes. There will be no more death or mourning or crying or pain, for the old order of things has passed away.'

I did not see a temple in the city, because the Lord God Almighty and the Lamb are its temple. The city does not need the sun or the moon to shine on it, for the glory of God gives it light, and the Lamb is its lamp. The nations will walk by its light, and the kings of the earth will bring their splendour into it. On no day will its gates ever be shut, for there will be no night there. The glory and honour of the nations will be brought into it. Nothing impure will ever enter it, nor will anyone who does what is shameful or deceitful, but only those whose names are written in the Lamb's book of life. (Revelation 21:1-4; 22-27)

It is important to notice the new element in Revelation that is not present in the Old Testament. The new element is 'the Lamb'. This Lamb, we were told in earlier chapters, was a lamb who has been slain but had risen to life so that he was standing (Revelation 5). It is this that makes the Jerusalem goal possible. Jerusalem as the place of God's dwelling with humanity is only possible because Jesus lived, died, and rose again.

FOR STUDY, DISCUSSION AND PRAYER

1. What similarities or differences are there between the stories of Daniel 3 and 6?

2. How should the godly respond to persecution for the sake of the gospel? Compare your answers with those given in 1 Peter 2-4.

3. What are the characteristics of Babylon (that is, the human city or kingdom) and Jerusalem (that is, God's city or kingdom)? How do we identify with God's city?

15

Shutting the Mouths of Lions 6:11-28

1. Closing the trap

(a) . . . On Darius

As Daniel prayed thanking God for the salvation which would come from Jerusalem, his executioners approached *as a group*. As predicted, they *found Daniel praying and asking God for help* as he had done countless times before. They returned *to the king* and *spoke to him* about his own law as children do with parents before trapping them in their own commitments: *'Did you not publish a decree that during the next thirty days anyone who prays to any god or man except you, O king, would be thrown into the lions' den?'*

The king answered them: *'The decree stands – in accordance with the laws of the Medes and the Persians, which cannot be repealed.'*

Then they said to the king, 'Daniel, who is one of the exiles from Judah, pays no attention to you, O king, or to the decree which you put in writing. He still prays three times a day.'

The words of the conspirators were carefully structured. Rather than referring to Daniel by his title and status, the conspirators reminded the king that he was in fact *one of the exiles;* a prisoner of war. Furthermore, he did not simply disregard the decree but paid *no attention to you, O king;* his personal allegiance was suspect. Daniel was painted as a complete traitor to the king.

It appears as though Daniel's piety was well known. There was no effort at verification. Instead the king was seized with distress and he *determined to rescue Daniel and make every effort . . . to save him.* But the trap jerked shut and the officials spoke. As a group they came before the king and reminded him of the law he himself set: *'Remember, O king, that according to the law of the Medes and Persians no decree or edict that the king issues can be changed.'*

Their words, cast in the imperative and showing no hint of politeness to the king, establish the king as one ensnared by his own edict and entangled by his own decree. Two victims, the king and Daniel squirmed under the weight of the courtiers' envy. The order went out and Daniel was brought and thrown into the lions' den.

2. In With The Lions

Lions were well known in Daniel's world. They roamed from Asia Minor through the Middle East and Persia to India. Daniel had probably watched them in that sport of kings, the lion hunt. The beaters would drive the quarry towards the hunters where, maddened by the attacks of the hounds and beaters they would always be eager to fight, but would do so uselessly against the arrows and spears of their assailants. Perhaps he had seen the proud animals in their death agonies and stepped across ground strewn with their bodies and blood while the day's bag was reckoned before the inevitable partying after the hunt.

The efforts of Darius came to nothing and so *the king gave the order, and they brought Daniel and threw him into the lions' den. The king said to Daniel, 'May your God, whom you serve continually, rescue you!'*

The statement rang with respect, displeasure and pathos. Daniel had the courage to be loyal to his God at any cost, even though Darius undoubtedly suspected him of being misguided in his allegiance. If Daniel had been faithful to the king instead of faithful to his God then he would not have been in this situation. The lions would not have been breathing down his neck.

Daniel had probably heard the screams of men and women and the roars of the lions as they had their day against humans and were victorious. Victims were torn limb from limb in a den of lions kept alive by the kings whom Daniel had served, for the purpose of carrying out judgment on their opponents. When *a stone was brought and placed over the mouth of the den*, and when *the king sealed it with his own signet ring and with the ring of his nobles*, Daniel knew what awaited him and did not demand deliverance. He knew God and would not give up that knowledge even to avoid the gaping, loathsome jaws of a lion.

As for the king, he spent *the night without eating and without any entertainment being brought to him. He could not sleep.*

3. Deliverance!

There were surprises for Daniel when he was thrown into the den. The starving beasts did not roar or tear him to pieces. Instead they lay down with him. As it will be in the future day of salvation promised by Isaiah, lions refused to act the part of carnivores. In the same way as they will refrain from violence one day on Mt Zion, they neither harmed nor destroyed on this night (cf Isaiah 11:6-9).

After breaking his own law, the law of the Medes and the Persians, by calling upon Daniel's God (6:16), the king who demanded allegiance to his kingship *at the first light of dawn...*

hurried to the lions den in anguish. He called out, confessing the power of Daniel's God: *'Daniel, servant of the living God, has your God, whom you serve continually, been able to rescue you from the lions?'*

As a true servant of the living God, the only King, and of the temporary king, Darius, Daniel replied. There was no anguish in his voice. It was calm, polite and full of courtly protocol as he explained: *'O king, live for ever! My God sent his angel, and he shut the mouths of the lions. They have not hurt me, because I was found innocent in his sight. Nor have I ever done any wrong before you, O king.'*

Daniel was unequivocal. God had rescued, and he had done so for two reasons. He was saved because of the blamelessness of his service in God's sight (no matter what the king thought of him!) and because of his faith in his God. Through faith the mouths of lions had been stopped (cf Hebrews 11:33).

This is reinforced by the next verse. *The king was overjoyed and gave orders to lift Daniel out of the den. And when Daniel was lifted from the den, no wound was found on him, because he had trusted in his God.*

In the lion's den Daniel was vindicated. By closing the mouths of the lions God was saying 'Daniel you have made the right choice and you are vindicated. You are free. Not only that, my law is vindicated. My law is **the** law and therefore I am vindicated.'

This is the real significance of the incident and of the story as a whole. Daniel was vindicated. He was righteous and innocent. The law of God was vindicated. It was and remains the true law. God was vindicated. He proved again, he was the greatest God. The words of Darius confirm this:

> *For he is the living God and he endures forever; his Kingdom will not be destroyed, his dominion will never end. He rescues*

*and he saves; he performs signs and wonders in the heavens and
on the earth. He has rescued Daniel from the power of the lions.*

In keeping with Persian practices, death and punishment
of courtiers and families was carried out and the fate which
they planned for Daniel became their fate. *At the king's
command, the men who had falsely accused Daniel were brought in
and thrown into the lion's den, along with their wives and children.
And before they reached the floor of the den, the lions overpowered
them and crushed all their bones.*

The fate of these men is also understandable given what
they had done to Darius. These men subverted his power
and made a fool of him. They had to be punished.

At the same time, Darius issued another decree
acknowledging the overarching kingship of Daniel's God and
his power, ability, life and salvation. Again Daniel *prospered,*
surviving because of his faith in a God who can shut the
mouths of lions.

As we have noted previously, Darius was most probably
one and the same person as Cyrus. Verse 28 should therefore
probably be translated as the NIV margin suggests: *So Daniel
prospered during the reign of Darius, that is, the reign of Cyrus the
Persian.*

4. Do Not Miss The Patterns!

Daniel knew the experience of his friends. In common
with his friends, he had paid the cost. As with them God was
faithful and remained present with him as he suffered. Just
as his friends had experienced deliverance, so did Daniel.
God rescued him.

What we learn from this episode of Daniel's life and from
the experiences of his friends is that:

- Belief in God costs something.

Being in relationship with God has all the benefits, demands and costs of being in any relationship. Being in relationship with him is not just about reaping the benefits but also about fulfilling the demands of loyalty and fidelity. It is about paying the cost of being allied with someone of whom the whole world is set against. Friendship with God means enmity with the world (James 4:4).

• The presence of God is assured at all times.

God has promised us that because we are related to him he will be faithful to us. Not to be faithful would be to deny himself (cf 2 Timothy 2:13) To desert us in our hour of need would mean admitting that he is unable to save and rescue, which in turn would mean admitting that he is not God.

• God will vindicate himself and us.

We are in relationship with a real and living God. While this is apparent to us, it is not always apparent to those around us. God promises that a day will come when he will vindicate himself and us. He will be seen for who he is and we shall be seen for our relationship to him.

To these three points some would add a fourth:

• God will rescue.

There is truth and falsehood about this statement. If by this statement we mean that God will always rescue us from the present difficulties in which we find ourselves because of our faith, then the statement is false. Even in the book of Daniel it is not true. While God does sometimes rescue his people from trouble and perform miraculous acts of deliverance (cf Daniel 1, 3, 6) or signs and wonders (cf Daniel 6:27), he does not always do so in this life.

As we shall see, one of the points of Daniel 7-12 is that the people of God are not always miraculously rescued. They suffer and die under persecution. They are beaten, tortured and mistreated. When this happens it is not because of their lack of faith. On the contrary, these people are people of extreme faith and perseverance.

The truth of the statement is found in its ultimate point of reference. God will finally rescue. He will rescue from the great enemy which Daniel, Shadrach, Meshach and Abednego faced. That great enemy is death. He may occasionally do it now, but for most of us he will do it in the way he did it for the saints of Daniel 7-12, in the resurrection of the dead (Daniel 12:1-3). This is the great rescue and it is a rescue which is assured.

Putting all this together, the overarching message of Daniel 6 is that God is faithful. It is not, 'Given this situation, God will change the circumstances'. Rather it is the message that, 'Given this situation, arrived at because of your faithfulness to your God, be assured of his faithfulness to you. He will never leave you nor forsake you.'

However, there are some other significant elements in this passage. When combined with Daniel 3 we notice a distinct pattern. The pattern turns up in the following areas.

(a) A Pattern For The People Of God

The pattern here is evident. God's people believed in God. They were in relationship with him and gave him their primary allegiance. They were faithful to him no matter what happened. They turned to him in prayer and dependence constantly and made active, practical choices to obey.

(b) A Pattern For The World

Again the passages speak lucidly. In the world encountered by the people of God there were and always will be those who sympathise with them and those who hate them. The people of God will undoubtedly meet up with those who will scheme, betray, take advantage of them and even persecute them. This was and is the way of the world.

(c) A Pattern For The Activity Of God

Finally, we have seen how the passages speak about God. The God of these passages is one who was active, who heard the voice of his people, was aware of their pain and suffering, entered into their world and got alongside them. He is a God who suffers with his people, remains faithful to them, vindicates and rescues them and finally triumphs through them.

5. Fulfilled in Jesus

These patterns are not new ones. We have seen them before in the Old Testament in such figures as Joseph and David (see especially his Psalms). They were also illustrated in the lives of such people as Esther. Of course we saw them most clearly demonstrated for us in the ministry of Jesus.

Like Daniel, Jesus was faithful to his relationship with God and to the task God had given him and this faithfulness made him a prime target for envy, leaving him exposed and vulnerable. Caiaphas, the chief priests and religious authorities took advantage of him. They decided to trap him by bringing his fidelity to his own mission into conflict with other laws and customs, knowing which he would choose (Matthew 26:57-68). Later they reported his messianic claims, thus throwing him into open conflict with the state (Matthew 27:11).

Jesus was also betrayed by those close to him and, like Daniel, on the eve of his arrest he did what all the saints of God do in such situations, he prayed (Matthew 26:36-55). When Jesus was brought before Pilate, Pilate sympathised with him and his plight as much as he was able, recognising his innocence and working for his release (Matthew 26:11ff). A centurion (Matthew 27:54) and a thief on the cross (Luke 24:40) also sympathised with him, recognising his faithfulness and innocence.

Nevertheless, Jesus paid the cost for his faithfulness to God. He was sentenced to death, mocked, executed and thrown into a tomb (Matthew 27:27ff). He was not rescued from the cross. On the contrary, God appeared to have abandoned him (Matthew 27:45-50). The promise of the divine presence in suffering was withdrawn because he bore our sin. However, after a period of three days, he was vindicated. God brought him back to life because of his innocence and faithfulness (Matthew 28:1ff). Jesus was vindicated. God was vindicated and his purposes were vindicated and fulfilled.

The course of history demonstrates these patterns. The faithfulness of the people of God to their God will always be taken advantage of, always bring them into suffering, and always bring them through to vindication. The faithfulness of the people of God will always be met by the faithfulness of God himself. God is God. God is faithful. God delivers.

This pattern has always been followed. It always will be followed. Jesus knew this, expected it, waited for it, and counted on it.

Daniel's emergence from what was to be his tomb in Daniel 6 was a symbol of resurrection. He was the wise man who arose from the dust of the earth to everlasting life and who shone forever like the brightness of the heavens (cf Daniel 12:1-4).

As noted before, the resurrection of Jesus was the vindication of Jesus and of God. However, it is more than this. It is also the symbol and assurance of our ultimate rescue and vindication, the guarantee that God will eventually do with us what he did with Jesus. The

133

resurrection is a guarantee that death has no sting. It is not a place of defeat, but of victory.

> When the perishable has been clothed with the imperishable and the mortal with immortality, then the saying that is written will come true: 'Death has been swallowed up in victory.'
>
> Where, O death, is your victory? Where, O death, is your sting?
>
> The sting of death is sin, and the power of sin is the law. But thanks be to God! He gives us the victory through our Lord Jesus Christ. (1 Corinthians 15:54-57)

6. God's Patterns And Us

These patterns and assurances are designed to be goads to us. Like those before us we are to remain faithful and immovable. We are to always give ourselves to our God and to his work knowing that our labour is not in vain (cf 1 Corinthians 15:58).

Like all people of faith, we are to look to the future, longing for a better world, a better country and a better city. We are to live in the Babylons of our world with our eyes and prayers fixed on another city with foundations, whose architect and builder is God (Hebrews 11:8-16). We are to maintain the faith, lining up with the great ones 'who through faith conquered kingdoms, administered justice, and gained what was promised; who shut the mouths of lions, quenched the fury of the flames, and escaped the edge of the sword; whose weakness was turned to strength' (Hebrews 11:33-34). Surrounded by them, we are to 'throw off everything that hinders and the sin that so easily entangles, and run with perseverance the race marked out for us. Let us fix our eyes on Jesus, the author and perfecter of our faith, who for the joy set before him endured the cross, scorning its shame, and sat down at the right hand of the throne of God. Consider him who endured such opposition from sinful men, so that you will not grow weary and lose heart.' (Hebrews 12:1-2).

However, the final word on this issue should go to the book of 1 Peter. This book is very similar to the first six chapters of Daniel. It was addressed to those who are God's own people (2:9-10) but who are exiles and sojourners in the world (1:1). It urged them to act as God's people in a world set against them (chapters 2 and 3), warning that this would result not only in glory being given to God, but also in suffering. Chapter 4 told them to be ready to suffer and not to be surprised when it comes. Chapter 5 finished with some comments which seem to have definite reference to Daniel 6.

> Humble yourselves, therefore, under God's mighty hand, that he may lift you up in due time. Cast all your anxiety on him because he cares for you. Be self-controlled and alert. Your enemy the devil prowls around like a roaring lion looking for someone to devour. Resist him, standing firm in the faith, because you know that your brothers throughout the world are undergoing the same kind of sufferings.

> And the God of all grace, who called you to his eternal glory in Christ, after you have suffered for a little while, will himself restore you and make you strong, firm and steadfast. To him be the power for ever and ever. Amen. (1 Peter 5:6-11)

Faith, humility, godly living and courage are fundamental ingredients of Christian life. They must be part of our make-up. Christianity is not an undertaking for the faint-hearted. It throws us into battle, bringing us under threat from all quarters. Books like Daniel and 1 Peter urge us on, saying to us, 'Endure! Be obedient at all costs! God will vindicate you! He always has and he always will.'

FOR STUDY, DISCUSSION AND PRAYER

1. List the similarities and differences between the story in Daniel 6 and that of Jesus in the last few chapters in Matthew's gospel.

2. What assurances do we have from God in the stories of Daniel 3 and 6 as to how he will act when we are persecuted and suffer because of our faith?

3. Read Hebrews 11:1-12:3. List the characteristics and implications of living by faith. What is the connection between chapter 11 and 12:1-3?

16

One Like a Son of Man 7:1-14

1. Pondering The Reign Of Belshazzar

With this chapter we return to *the first year of Belshazzar king of Babylon*. This was probably around 550 BC when Nabonidus was away and Belshazzar operated as co-regent. It was also probably the year in which Cyrus took over the Median empire on his way to the eventual overthrow of Babylon.

These last days of the Babylonian kingdom were days of hope for many of Daniel's fellow Israelites. They began to expect deliverance at the hand of the new and up-coming kingdom of the Medes and Persians. Daniel 7 delved into Daniel's dream world and demonstrated that he did not share the optimism of his fellow country people.

It was not surprising that Daniel was more cautious. After all, Genesis 6 told us that 'every inclination of the thoughts of man's heart is only on evil all the time' (Genesis 6:5) and the existence of Nebuchadnezzar's strange dream regarding future kingdoms (Daniel 2), indicated that things would get worse before they got better. Although the long-term future was not under doubt, the nearer future might not be as promising as some had hoped.

Chapters 7 to 12 of Daniel seem to concentrate on this. They ponder a whole different set of questions, such as: 'What would happen when things were no longer bearable, when the malice, arrogance and resentment of pagan kings could no longer be handled by the people of God? What would happen when persecution became unbearable? How could the people of God face a world where they were no longer rescued, where the flames consumed them and the lions tore them apart? If things did get worse, how could they be grappled with? How could God be explained? How could he be lived for in a world like that?'

Given the nature of Belshazzar's reign it is not surprising that these question began to be posed *in the first year of Belshazzar king of Babylon.*

2. The Prophet Who Dreamed

With his mind deeply rooted in the writings of the law, prophets and wise men, as well as his own experience, Daniel retired one night. As he slept, he *had a dream, and visions passed through his mind as he was lying on his bed.*

Daniel's dream was recorded for us, for *he wrote down the substance of his dream.*

His dream was of the sea. Gales came from every direction, coming as a whirlwind over the deep, murky blue waters, arousing them into a turbulent swell of heaving, foam-tipped waves. Supernatural winds whipped up the sea, agitating and stirring them. Then from the midst of its depths, out of chaos, emerged four creatures which were powerful, threatening and increasingly sinister. This was the stuff of nightmares.

138

(a) The Watery Chaos

In verse three we are told that *four great beasts, each different from the others, came up out of the sea.* The *sea* or 'the deep' was an element which was dwelt on much by the prophets and poets of Israel and it was undoubtedly their writings which influenced the images and language used by Daniel.

(i) Something to be feared

As a land-based people the Jews saw the sea as a most formidable and unpredictable element, a place of dark, deep waters and strange creatures. Dense, hostile and dangerous, it represented a concentration of energy which split people apart and threatened to disrupt and overwhelm order.

(ii) A tameable force

However, the Scriptures gave another picture of the sea and the supposedly fearful things that dwelt in its watery chaos. The sea was the creation of God. In the beginning, God had created the heavens and the earth. He had tamed the chaotic deep seas, separating them and naming them (Genesis 1:1-10). He had founded the earth upon the seas and established it upon the rivers (Psalm 24:1). Therefore not even the sea was outside his creative genius and sovereignty. The sea was his, for he made it. In his hands were the depths of the earth (Psalm 95:4-5 cf Psalm 104:1-9).

(iii) A cause for wonder and praise

According to the Scriptures, the sea ought not to arouse fear, but wonder and praise (Psalm 148:7ff). Those who go down to the sea in ships and sail on it should not fear, but watch and see the works of the Lord, his wonderful deeds in the deep. As they rise and fall to the motion of the waves they are to wonder at the fact that as he speaks the waves mount up to the heavens and go down to the depths. As he utters his word the waves are stilled and the sea is hushed (Psalm 107:23-32).

As for the animals and monsters which fill the waterways of the deep, they are not loosed gods, but creatures of the Creator God, Yahweh. Even Leviathan, the mythical sea creature, is not independent or outside Yahweh's control. On the contrary, he is put there by God for frolic and play. All the world, and all in it are subject to God, even the sea and its host. All of it depends on him, relying on him to give what is needed for life and sustenance (cf Psalm 104:19-30).

Because of this sort of thinking the sea was often used by the prophets and poets of Israel to represent the forces of chaos arrayed against God. It was a good metaphor for although it looked out of control, in reality it stood under the sovereign rule of God. In similar manner, the nations often arrayed themselves against God, appearing to be out of control but in reality they and their actions were well within the plan and purposes of Yahweh. This is the significance of the image used by Daniel in this passage. These beasts which emerged from the sea were seemingly unruly and out of control, however, Daniel 2 taught that they were in reality under the sovereign rule of Yahweh and his goal for history.

(b) The Creatures Arrayed Against God (7:1-8)

(i) One like a lion

The first creature to emerge from the sea was like a lion, the king of the animal world. Reminiscent of Nebuchadnezzar's hair like eagle's feathers, this beast had wings like those of an eagle, the king of the bird world. In his dream, Daniel was captivated by it, unable to shift his eyes from it. Then, as he watched, its huge and glorious *wings were torn off and it was lifted from the ground so that it stood on two feet like a man, and the heart of a man was given to it.* Again, the correspondences between Nebuchadnezzar and the beast cannot be missed.

Daniel would have recognised Nebuchadnezzar. He would have recognised the beastly in him. At such times he refused to stand under the overarching rule of God and he was arrogant and boastful. As well he would have recognised the human in him, those moments when he had looked and acted like a man in the image of God, ruling under the kingship of God and carrying out the will of God for his creation.

(ii) One like a bear

Then, as he dreamed, his focus shifted. There beside the sea was a *second beast.* It too was terrifying, resembling *a bear*, huge, voracious and malignant in its use of strength, the most dreaded animal known in Palestine. Reared up on its hind legs, it had one paw ready to strike out at any in its path. With *three ribs* remaining *in its mouth* from its last bloody repast, it was told by a voice from out of the dark, *'Get up and eat your fill of flesh!'*

It is tempting to try and identify each of these beasts and although there are some likely candidates for each, we should probably rather take in the broader picture. For example, we should note the thrust of this image of the bear was on its voracious appetite. Here was a nation with a hunger for expansion and an increase of its rule. The vision tells us that such horrifying expansionism can even be under the control of God. It may be under his direction, and part of his larger purpose that the beast gets up and eats its fill of flesh.

(iii) One like a leopard

Thirdly, he saw before him another beast, a fearsome predator, looking *like a leopard*. It too had *wings*, like the first beast. This time there were *four* of them attached to its back, along with *four heads* on its shoulders. Because of its wings, head and eyes it was able to see everywhere and move quickly and ably in any direction. Like the others, this beast was *given authority to rule*. Like the others, this beast was terrifying and beastly in its exercise of that rule.

(iv) One too frightening for words

Then came the *fourth beast*, so *frightening* that it could not be explained. No beast known to Daniel resembled it. *Terrifying* and sinister in the extreme it crawled from the sea with huge torrents of water streaming from its back. With *large iron teeth it crushed and devoured its victims* before marching on remorselessly, trampling over the remnants of its victims as it went, explicitly fearsome and destructive.

Ten horns, symbols of full-blown strength and power protruded from the head of this beast and while Daniel pondered them he saw *another horn* emerge. This horn was *little* and *came up* in the midst of the other ten. Then, before his eyes, *three of the first horns were uprooted before it*. As Daniel peered closer he noticed *the eyes of a man and a mouth* which spewed out boastful, godless words.

The first three animals were clearly under control. Not so with this beast. It took on a mind of its own, doing its own thing, its own way, without God. It was destructive, arrogant and godless. Instead of living under the rule and purpose of God's history it overreached itself and attempted to take control of its own destiny. It took on God, assaulting the people of God, crushing and defeating them.

The importance of the four beasts is that human rule can look like this. On the one hand it is under the control of God and directed by him. On the other hand, it can look totally out of his control and under the control of human sinfulness and arrogance.

Just as the first beast strongly reminded us of Nebuchadnezzar, the first pagan king to rule the nation of Israel, so the last beast reminds us of the pinnacle of Greek rule over the nation of Israel. In this case the *ten horns* would symbolically represent royal rule rounded out rather than ten specific kings. The small horn, however, probably has reference to a particular Seleucid king, Antiochus IV, otherwise known as Antiochus Epiphanes. It was this king who won notoriety as the most vicious and out of control ruler since the exile under Nebuchadnezzar.

It was also Antiochus Epiphanes who forced his way onto his throne and who tried to *change the set times and the laws* (7:25). This reference to *set times*, while possibly referring to his attempts to replace the 365 day solar calendar by a 360 day lunar calendar, is more probably referring to his defiance of the proper course of history (cf the similar usage in 2:21 where God *changes times and seasons; he sets up kings and deposes them*). Similarly, the reference to *laws* in 7:25 could be talking about Jewish laws, but is perhaps better understood as a reference to God's decree of judgment on him. In this case, the dream tells us that although Antiochus assumed the position of God and tried to change and control history, his attempts were in vain.

Although he had been given authority to rule (that is, although he has *eyes like the eyes of a man*), Antiochus lifted himself up before God and spoke boastfully against him, seemingly taking the control of history and his own destiny into his own hands.

(c) A Court Open For Business (7:9-14)

It was at this point, when human rule was at its most arrogant and when it was seemingly out of control that, without warning, *thrones were set in place* ready for the inevitable divine judgment.

As Daniel looked there was no horror nor fear, no turbulent wind, crashing of waves nor crushing, flying, stomping beasts. Instead of chaos there was order and dignity. Serenely God, *the Ancient of Days, took his seat. His clothing was as white as snow, the hair of his head was white like wool. His throne* flamed *with fire* and *its wheels were ablaze.* Before him there flowed a *river of fire* and *thousands upon thousands attended him, ten thousand upon ten thousand stood before him.* Then the heavenly court sat down. *The books were opened* and all waited for judgment to be proclaimed.

Just as the Scriptures had calmed his fears of the sea earlier, this vision of Yahweh would have calmed Daniel's dismay concerning the beasts emerging from the sea. It was a vision of God in control. God had a course set for history. He would judge those who did not rule and act under his kingly rule, entering into combat with opposing forces of chaos, bringing them to account. History may proceed in such a way as to appear without pattern and meaning. The nations may seem to be autonomous and out of control but in reality, God was not asleep nor absent. God was reigning and judging.

Despite the comfort of the vision Daniel continued to hear the *boastful*, insistent, provocative voice echoing from the tiny mouth of the little *horn*. He turned to look and as he watched *the beast was slain, its body destroyed and thrown into the blazing fire.*

At this point an aside was made and we are told that *the other beasts had been stripped of their authority, but were allowed to live for a period of time.* These words should warn us against being too strict in our identification of the various beasts depicted in the vision. They tell us that whoever the original beasts stood for, their kingdoms and the nature of their rule continue to be recognisable in history. As in Daniel 2, they will fall with the fall of the fourth kingdom, at the end of history. The words *for a period of time* imply that their future is limited, God will not allow it to continue forever. There will be an end to such rule.

While still gazing at the destruction of the beast Daniel's attention was arrested by a most amazing event. In his vision of the night another figure emerged. This was no beast. It had no animal features. There were no deep, dark, recesses here, but only light. It came as *one like a Son of Man*, a human figure. At the same time it was a heavenly figure, not an earthly one. Boldly this one approached the court-room and was led into the presence of the Ancient of Days. Once there he was handed a kingdom, given authority and sovereign power. All peoples, nations and men of every language worshipped him, for his dominion was an everlasting dominion that would not pass away. His kingdom was one which would not be destroyed.

It is important not to miss the contrast here. Here was a human being, one in the image of God, who was at the same time a heavenly figure who ruled like man was meant to rule, that is, under the rule of God. The contrast occurs at a number of levels: chaos versus order, beastly versus human, temporary versus eternal, seized versus given, condemned versus endorsed. Here was something Daniel and many others had longed and waited for since Adam's failure. One who lived out the divine rule of God.

(d) One Like A Son Of Man

It is important to make some preliminary points about this enigmatic 'Son of Man'. This commentary has taken the position that the term needs to be understood within the framework of the whole book and within the framework of the book's understanding of the kingdom of God.

When we looked at the earlier chapters of Daniel we learnt that there were two kinds of rule:

- rule which was human in nature (that is, rule which ruled under the overarching rule of God, in the image of God as intended, see Genesis 1:27-28 and Psalm 8); and

- rule which was animal or beastly in nature (that is, rule which ruled with humanity at its centre and in independence of the overarching rule of God).

We learnt that while some rulers sometimes ruled in the image of God, and therefore could be represented in human terms such as Nebuchadnezzar was in chapter 4 and then again in verse 4 of this chapter, none ruled perfectly and many preferred to rule as beasts. The Son of Man is therefore one who rules as 'a man' (that is, in the image of God, under the overarching rule of God) perfectly. Such a person is fit to be given all authority and sovereign power, for he is able to do what none have done. He is perfect man, one truly in the image of God, a new and perfect Adam.

The difficulty is that this figure is not just a man. He came *on the clouds of heaven* and was able to approach the *Ancient of Days* and *be led into his presence.* He was not only *given authority, glory and sovereign power,* but *all peoples, nations and men of every language worshipped* him. He was a heavenly figure.

3. A God Who is In Control

We live in a world which looks out of control. We find ourselves caught in the vice-like grip of forces which seem way out of our control. While natural forces can sometimes be the culprit, they are not the ones we feel most acutely. The forces we feel most acutely are those which are human in origin: political, economic, social.

As those who have the world brought into our lounge room with modern technology we are well aware of political kingdoms like each of the beasts listed in Daniel 7. Even today some of the nations of the world liken themselves, or are likened, to beasts of prey (eagles, bears, etc.). Some rule well, even humanely and some are voracious and expansionist and some are swift to gain power but short-lived. Others are arrogant, cruel, boastful and apparently out of control.

Economic forces also buffet us and put us at the beck and call of interest rates and dollar values. Economic manipulation is done by men and women with faces we do not know and names we never hear and the market rises or falls at their whim. Again, it is a world which seems out of our control.

Social policy is enacted which may or may not help the poor and disadvantaged and which may or may not grasp the nettles that overgrow our society. We feel overwhelmed, unable to act, powerless to influence and change such policy. After all, who are we in this world of super-powers and super-people?

The word of Daniel for us is that there is a God who is in control of the seemingly uncontrollable. There is an Ancient of Days who is seated in judgment and before whom books are opened. He has a plan and purpose for his world and he will assuredly bring it to pass. We may not perceive his presence, but he is not asleep or absent. He is reigning and judging. In contrast to chaos he will bring order. In contrast to beastly human rule he will bring human rule as it was intended. It will be eternal rather than temporary, given rather than seized and endorsed rather than condemned.

FOR STUDY, DISCUSSION AND PRAYER

1. What is the significance of 'the first year of Belshazzar, king of Babylon' in Daniel 7?

2. How would what the Scripture says about the sea help Daniel understand and come to grips with the dream recorded in Daniel 7?

3. Why does the writer use the term 'Son of Man' at this point in the book? What is meant to be conveyed?

4. Spend some time reflecting on the portrait of God given in the chapter. Use this as the basis of a time of prayer, praising God for his character.

5. What are the issues and difficulties that cause the most concern in our world? What does Daniel 7 have to say to our world on these matters?

17

Pondering Dreams and Visions 7:15-28

1. Pondering the Dream

As Daniel dreamed, he was *troubled in spirit*. Some of the details of *the visions that passed though* his *mind disturbed* and confused him. In his vision he *approached one of those standing* nearby and questioned him as to *the true meaning* of what he had seen.

(a) The Beasts and the Son of Man

The explanation of Daniel's dream was straightforward and clear in broad outline: *'The four great beasts are four kingdoms that will rise from the earth. But the saints of the Most High will receive the kingdom and will possess it forever – yes, for ever and ever.'*

Nebuchadnezzar's dream (Daniel 2) had taught Daniel to expect four kingdoms. There the dream had mentioned a 'rock cut out of the mountain, but not by human hands' which symbolised a kingdom which would never be destroyed and which would break the other kingdoms of iron, bronze, clay, silver and gold to pieces. In this dream also there was an eternal kingdom which would replace the kingdoms of this world, but there was also the additional element, the giving of this kingdom of God to a heavenly, human-like figure.

The overall thrust of Daniel's dream is understandable. Behind the world which Daniel knew and encountered each day, there was a heavenly, spiritual world. This was the world of reality. In this world of reality a heavenly battle was in full swing. On the one side were the anti-God forces of chaos and disorder, represented by the beasts from the sea and kingdoms of the world. These forces would become evident in the unfolding of history, in the rule of kings and rulers who would reject the rule of God and tyrannise the people of God.

Moreover, just as the sea met God and was forced to proclaim his goodness, sing his praises and be calm, so it would be with the forces of chaos, whether they were mythical creatures like Leviathan or Rahab or real kings such as Nebuchadnezzar. They would reap judgment and bow before the King of kings.

On the other side of the battle were the pro-God forces, represented by the saints of the Most High, who in turn were represented in heaven by the Son of Man coming on the clouds of heaven.

The court-room scene indicated that the result of the conflict was foreordained and already decided, not only for the losers but also for the winners. The saints of the Most High would win and receive the kingdom at the hands of their representative in heaven, this one like a Son of Man coming on the clouds of heaven. It had already been decided. God had decreed it.

(b) The Fourth Beast

Despite understanding the broad outline of the dream, Daniel craved further detail and so he pushed for more explanation as to *the true meaning of the fourth beast,* the one *which was different from all the others and most terrifying, with its iron teeth and bronze claws – the beast that crushed and devoured its victims and trampled underfoot whatever was left.* In addition, he *wanted to know about the ten horns on its head and the other horn that came up before which three of them fell.*

Daniel's interest was understandable apart from mere curiosity. After all, it was this *other horn* which he saw in his dream *waging war against the saints and defeating them.*

Again the explanation came:

> *The fourth beast is a fourth kingdom that will appear on earth. It will be different from all the other kingdoms and will devour the whole earth, trampling it down and crushing it. The ten horns are ten kings who will come from this kingdom. After them another king will arise, different from the earlier ones; he will subdue three kings. He will speak against the Most High and oppress his saints and try to change the set times and the laws. The saints will be handed over to him for a time, times and half a time.*

> *But the court will sit, and his power will be taken away and completely destroyed for ever. Then the sovereignty, power and greatness of the kingdoms under the whole heaven will be handed over to the saints, the people of the Most High. His kingdom will be an everlasting kingdom, and all rulers will worship and obey him.*

At this point Daniel's anxiety deepened. He was *deeply troubled* and his *face turned pale.* Daniel knew now that his pessimism regarding the near future was warranted. Dark days were ahead for the people of God, dark days in which their only comfort was that there will be a limitation applied (*the saints will be handed over to him for a time, times and half a time,* 7:25). Eventually there will be a day when wrong will be righted, God will reign, and his people will reign with him over a world in submission to him, but before that time there was cause for fear...

2. Literature For Troubled Times

(a) A Particular Brand Of Literature

Daniel 7 is markedly different from chapters 1-6. It is part of a style of literature which began to appear around about the time of the exile and which continued through to the New Testament. Called 'apocalyptic' by biblical scholars, it was a literature composed in or for times of trial as a kind of private comfort for believers. It was written with the realisation that things are not always right on earth and that the people of God are not always victorious and kept safe. As you read the Old Testament (and the New Testament) you will find pockets of it tucked away in such places as the middle of the book of Isaiah (chapters 24-27), in Ezekiel 37-39, and in Joel (or Mark 13 and 2 Thessalonians 2). Daniel 7-12 is the first full-blown expression of such literature. The last example we have in our Bibles is the book of Revelation.

(b) A Philosophy Of Life And History

Apocalyptic was not only a form of writing. It was also a philosophy of life and history, a world view. Fundamental to its thinking was that history moves in regular, recurring patterns or waves of events, spiralling toward the point where God will finally burst in upon history in a dramatic way to wind up history, judge those in opposition, and vindicate those faithful to him. What apocalyptic was saying was that this is how the world runs. This is how circumstances always turn out in the world over which God is sovereign. Given such and such an event, such and such will follow.

(c) Apocalyptic and Daniel 7

We can see this in Daniel 7. We are shown that there are historical forces which sweep through this world every now and then. They are forces which are anti-God and which therefore scar the people of God. However, God is the king of the world and therefore in control. He has always defeated and judged the forces of chaos. He did it in creation, and he will always do it. Therefore the saints should be aware that although things are grim for them, their reward is a sure reward. God will win. Opposing world forces have already been judged and condemned in heaven and this decision will be seen in history. It will surely be carried out.

Moreover, the saints will receive a kingdom from God. They do not know when, but what they do know is that things will get worse before they get better and that final vindication will not come until after the worst of the forces of evil have been overcome. Their receiving a kingdom will be associated with the coming of the Ancient of Days to judge.

The glimpse into the heavenly courts assures the reader under the stress of persecution that the world has already been judged for its resistance to God. With the approach of one like a Son of Man the judgment process is loosed on history. This is what Daniel saw.

The stoning of Stephen in Acts 7 helps us understand this. As he was being stoned, Stephen looked up and saw the Son of Man standing in judgment. The Son of Man, representative of the people of God, was standing and already pronouncing judgment. In effect he was saying, 'I have seen, Stephen. I have judged, and you are vindicated. Historical processes may sweep over this world, scarring people of God like you, but the reward of God is sure. Opposing world systems have already been condemned. The decision of the heavenly court, my decision, must simply be brought to bear on this particular historical case.'

The Most High is the reigning king of heaven and earth. There is opposition from chaos and anti-God forces. It is formidable opposition. It is fierce and harsh. However, the Most High is in control all the time and even though his opponents are successful for a little while he will win in the long run.

(d) The Message Of Apocalyptic

These are great truths from a world view which is strong and vibrant. Apocalyptic was realistic and freely admitted that the world was not as it should be. Suffering and pain, satanic power and victories by the kings of this earth were real. On the other hand it looked beyond the present and it pronounced a greater reality. It said, 'There are books already opened in heaven. Beyond this world there is a God who is just, who judges, who is in control, and who orders human concerns. Put your faith in him! Before long this world will reflect what he has already decided. Soon the tyrants of this world will meet their pre-ordained fate and the saints of this world will collect their pre-ordained kingdom.'

For all its obscurity and fascinating, terrifying figures, the message shone through: although successive kings and kingdoms have acted arrogantly against God, treating God's people in brutal ways and in brutish fashion, they can only go so far. One day they will have to face divine retribution. On such a day it will not be enough to chastise and curb their power, they will need to be utterly destroyed before the coming kingdom of God. In their place God will set up his kingdom. He will delegate the rule of that kingdom to the faithful among his people, represented by the Son of Man.

Beyond this, by letting us behind the scenes and showing us another, spiritual world the writers tell us plainly that there are kings that will come upon this world who will embody a power of incredible magnitude. The source of such power and evil can only be supernatural in its evil and chaos. It can be nothing short of satanic.

Apocalyptic literature therefore spanned many ages and spoke in general principles. Its impact would have been to assure its hearers that as the people of God suffered under unjust and domineering rulers they could be assured that there was another, just King, under whose rule history was not out of control. The outcome of history rests in the hands of a merciful and just judge and not in the hands of persecutors and the unjust.

As a result apocalyptic literature proclaimed that there was no terror in history. There are no unique, unrepeatable events. The struggle is as old as the battle against the sea and all that dwells in it and is as assured as Yahweh's victory over them.

As for the relevance of such a message for us, it bursts from the pages of all apocalyptic literature. God is in control and that meaning for life finds its source and focus in heaven with him. Therefore, as life is met, be aware of another world, a world ruled by the King of heaven who is concerned about you and what you are experiencing. This world is a world in which judgment has already been announced and proclaimed, in which God has been, is, and will be victorious. Such may not be immediately evident to you, but if you care to lift your eyes to heaven you will see it. This is the world where reality is found.

Therefore saints in all ages are not to lose heart as they look at the world and at the persecution it thrusts upon them. Though outwardly they are wasting away, inwardly they are being renewed day by day. Their light (!) and momentary troubles as they struggle to be faithful to their God are achieving for them an eternal glory which far outweighs them all. They are to fix their eyes not on the things which are seen, but the things which are unseen. What is seen is temporary, but what is unseen is eternal (cf 2 Corinthians

4:7-18, especially verses 17-18). This is where reality is found, in heaven itself, not here on earth.

FOR STUDY, DISCUSSION AND PRAYER

1. Get a copy of the apocryphal books of 1 and 2 Maccabees. Read 1 Maccabees 1 and 2 Maccabees 4-9.

2. What are the characteristics of apocalyptic literature?

3. How does an understanding of apocalyptic literature help us understand Daniel 7-12?

4. What is the central message of Daniel 7?

18

Understanding the Kingdom of God (III)

1. The Kingdom and Being Wise

(a) Daniel and Wisdom Literature

In Jeremiah 18:18 we are told of three groups of 'experts' within Israel: the priest, the wise person, and the prophet. Each of these groups lies behind various writings of the Old Testament. Wisdom was an internationally known phenomena, practised in both Egypt and Babylon as well as Israel. Each had their wise men or sages. Within Israel we also hear of wise women (cf 2 Samuel 14:2ff). These wise people are responsible for such books as Job, Proverbs, Ecclesiastes and the Song of Solomon.

However, the influence of Israel's sages spread much more broadly than just these books and seemed to make inroads into other sorts of Israelite literature as well, such as the stories of Joseph, David, and Daniel.

(b) The Principal Characteristics Of Wisdom

(i)   Not via intellectual clarity

The first thing about wisdom is that it does not come via intellectual clarity or discrimination or astuteness of mind. True wisdom comes from the most unusual and unexpected source. It comes through religious commitment and the fear of the Lord (cf Proverbs 9:10). Therefore to fear the Lord is to be truly wise. It is to acknowledge that there is a basic premise that lies behind all of life and all which could be truly called 'wisdom', that the world occupied by human beings is a created one, a world which is first and foremost God's world.

(ii)   Demands a personal response

Secondly, the book of Proverbs teaches that wisdom challenges personally and individually. It made clear that each person in this world is presented with two invitations and that each person must hear and make an individual response. When they do, they also must bear the responsibility and consequences of their choice. The choice and consequences are evident: 'If you are wise, your wisdom will reward you; if you are a mocker, you alone will suffer' (Proverbs 9:12).

(iii) Is worked out in practical, everyday decisions

Finally, wisdom is about practical, everyday living. Wisdom is about letting your fear of God as the Creator of the universe affect the everyday. Wise people therefore need to be constantly making decisions, deciding how to express their commitment to God. When faced with the demands of the world and the demands of God they must fear God not humans and make practical decisions as to how they express that fear.

(c) Daniel the Wise Man

There is much evidence to suggest that in many ways, the book of Daniel presents Daniel as an ideal wise man who continually decided to fear God (that is, to be wise) rather than to ignore God due to the demands of others (that is, folly). The stories about Daniel are like the stories of Joseph. They are about living wisely in a world which continually calls people to folly. Daniel was one who constantly made decisions which were affected by his determination to fear God more than to fear humans.

(d) Chapters 4 and 5

We saw that the theme of wisdom intersects with the theme of the kingdom of God in chapters 4 and 5. In these two stories we saw that God wants all people to see life and rule rightly. He wants people to be true human beings, fulfilling their function as the image of God as they were meant to fulfil it, under the overarching rule of God. In the words of wisdom, to be true human beings, seeing life and ruling in right perspective is to fear the Lord, respecting him, revering him and living life practically under his guidance and instruction. The beginning (and end!) of wisdom is the fear of the Lord.

Nebuchadnezzar came to realise this fact. He *'raised his eyes towards heaven'* and had his sanity restored, (that is, he saw reality).

Belshazzar was different. He was a fool, thinking and acting as though there was no God (Psalm 14:1). To be proud and autonomous is to be a fool, a mere animal. To be wise is to fear God. To be a fool is to sow the seed of your own destruction, as Belshazzar sowed. It is to face a day of reaping, as Belshazzar did.

It is these observations that allow us to add another building block in our understanding of the kingdom of God which links the idea of wisdom with the idea of the kingdom of God.

- Human beings can be divided into two groups:

The Wise: Those who recognise the overarching rule of God and live and rule under it.

The Foolish: Those who say in their heart, 'There is no God' and refuse to live and rule under his dominion.

Like Belshazzar, the fourth kingdom of chapter 7 is the kingdom of a fool who refused to acknowledge God and to live or rule under his sovereignty. He refused the wise approach to life which is to fear God and give him glory. His end will be destruction.

The saints, on the other hand, give God his right place. Their end will be vindication and salvation (cf Daniel 12:1-3)

2. The Kingdom and the Son of Man

(a) God's Goal For His World

Daniel 7 also helps us to understand more about another of our previous building blocks about the kingdom of God, that is,

- The kingship of God is headed toward a goal. The world living under God as King and the end of all rivals to his kingship.

In Daniel 7 we see God actually winding up history, judging it, and setting it right. However, the impact of Daniel 7 does not stop there. With the advent of *one like a Son of Man* and *the saints of the Most High* we have important further developments.

However, before we state these developments we need to do some background work. The term *one like a Son of Man* is important and we need to understand its meaning in its original context before we take the jump through to the first century. There are a few things to notice about the meaning of the term itself and its meaning in the context of the whole dream and the book as a whole.

- The immediate context tells us that whoever *one like a Son of Man* is, he is a heavenly figure.

- The interpretation of the dream clearly signified some correlation between *one like a Son of Man* and *the saints of the Most High*. In the dream it was *one like a Son of Man* who received the everlasting kingdom (7:13-14), while in the angelic interpretation it was *the saints of the Most High* who received the kingdom and possessed it forever (7:18 cf 7:27). *One like a Son of Man* therefore appeared to be a type of heavenly representative of the saints.

- The term *one like a Son of Man* meant something like 'a human-like figure' and as such operated as a strong contrast to the four great beasts. Human-like rule was set in opposition to beast-like rule.

- Genesis 1:27-28, Psalm 8, Daniel 2 and Daniel 4 form a necessary backdrop to our understanding of the term *one like a Son of Man*.

In Genesis 1 and Psalm 8 we see that to be in 'the image of God', that is, to be human, was to live in the world under the rule of God. This was the way God made humans.

Daniel 2, like Jeremiah 27:1-5, used the language of Genesis 1 and Psalm 8 to refer to Nebuchadnezzar and thereby made it clear that he was not autonomous. He was a created being and appointed by God as a ruler over his over world. As such he must rule humanly, that is, under the overarching rule of God.

Daniel 4 indicated that Nebuchadnezzar's rule was sometimes the way it was intended, but that at its roots it was set against God (it stood on feet of clay - Daniel 2). Although there were times in his life when he acted in the image of God (that is, humanly) by *lifting his eyes to heaven*, his reign was often arrogant and beastly in character.

This is picked up in Daniel 7. The first beast obviously symbolises the reign of Nebuchadnezzar. It is beastly in style, although at times it looks human. Such rule is given by God, but can only be temporary.

In contrast to this half beast, half human, there came *one like a Son of Man*. Here was a full human being, one who lived and ruled under the dominion of God. Only such a one as this was worthy to receive the eternal kingdom. He is representative of all those who are wise and poor in spirit as they recognise that God alone rules and they live in the light of this fact.

(b) Jesus And The Son Of Man

There is little doubt that the ultimate fulfilment of *one like a Son of Man* came in the Son of God. Jesus of Nazareth's favourite name for himself was 'the Son of Man'. When he came to earth and ministered he was obviously aware of Daniel 7 and its world of thought. He knew that there was a battle going on and that he was caught up in the midst of it; even that he was its focus. With him and in his ministry heaven stepped onto earth for a little while, and he waged war. He stilled the great watery chaos with his powerful word as it threatened to overpower the people of God (Mark 4:35-41). He walked on the surface of the water (Mark 6:45-52) as God himself walked in the recesses of the deep (Job 38.16). He urged his people to take courage and not be afraid at the raging of the sea (and perhaps symbolically at the raging of the nations – Mark 6:45-52).

He cast out the satanic forces of evil from people. He healed the sick. In effect he said, 'The finger of God has come upon you as I do this. I am showing you what happens in heaven, demonstrating the power of God and of his kingdom. I am letting you behind the scenes. I am the Son of Man who represents you before God.'

One like a Son of Man was where Jesus found his identity. Hence, when he was dragged before the authorities he said, 'You shall see the Son of Man coming on the clouds of heaven (that is, in judgment)'. Jesus knew that he represented and embodied the kingdom; that he represented and embodied the people of God. As he defeated Satan on the cross so the kingdom will be ours through his victory. He received the kingdom that we shall receive, all in fulfilment of Daniel 7.

(c) Jesus and Adam

Now we can see and understand why Jesus is the second Adam. He alone has perfectly lived under the overarching rule of God. He is the perfect man. He is therefore God's choice for the future. He is the one whom God has appointed as ruler of his everlasting kingdom.

As you can see, Daniel 7 helps us add a further explanatory note to our already existing knowledge about Jesus, and to increase our understanding of the kingdom of God in Daniel.

- There is only one who has exercised the rule of God perfectly, Jesus. He is given the rule of God for all time.

Also,

- He will in turn give the kingdom to the wise.

Daniel 4 and 5 told us that our God is one who rules the kingdoms of men, giving them to whom he will. Although 'whom he will' has first reference to Jesus, it does not stop there. God talks of other meek, humble, obedient human beings who have learnt to live as the image of God. He promises as such that they will inherit the earth (Matthew

5:5). He will exalt the lowliest of human beings and place them over the kingdoms of humankind (cf Daniel 4:17).

This is the promise to all obedient and loyal people of all generations. Those who are humble, lowly, dependent, lacking in any desire for autonomy will one day rule the kingdom that is so badly ruled now by others above them.

3. An End Time In-Sight

For us as Christians, then, Daniel 7 rolls back the heavens, urging us to take a peek into heaven, beckoning us to look and see that God is there. He is acting. He is fighting. He will be victorious. He is the one behind history.

There are situations where we shall need to know this truth, where we shall not understand our world and shall need to see God, his battle and his victory. We shall need to see that there is a victory which we cannot accomplish nor can any other person. However, there is a God who can and will be victorious.

And what should we do? How then should we live? The New Testament urges us in the following manner:

Therefore, stand firm. Let nothing move you. Always give yourselves fully to the work of the Lord, because you know that your labour in the Lord is not in vain.

(1 Corinthians 15:58; cf 2 Timothy 4:1-5; 2 Peter 3:10-13)

FOR STUDY, DISCUSSION AND PRAYER

1. List some of the principal characteristics of wisdom literature in the Old Testament. Think back on the stories of Daniel 1-6. Where do we see Daniel acting like a traditional Old Testament 'wise man'?

2. Read Proverbs 9. To whom is wisdom likened? To whom is folly likened? What are the characteristics of wisdom and folly? Where do a wise life end and a foolish life end?

3. How does Daniel 7 help us understand who Jesus is and what he has done? How did Jesus fulfil Daniel 7?

19

Reaching For Heaven 8:1-14

1. Isaiah 14

The writers of apocalyptic were primarily people of the Scriptures. They stood on the shoulders of the prophets and deeply imbibed their works. Daniel was no different. His waking thoughts and his dreams and visions were coloured by the writings of those prophets who had gone before him.

One prophecy particularly important for understanding Daniel 8 is Isaiah 14 which concerns the king of Babylon. It was a particularly apt prophecy for Daniel to be reflecting on for it was a taunt that was to be taken up 'on the day the Lord' gave 'relief from suffering and turmoil and cruel bondage' (Isaiah 14:3). The third year of Belshazzar was the same year in which Cyrus established the state of the Medes and the Persians and speculations regarding this rising star must have been rife. Many would have hoped that the day of relief from suffering in Babylon might not be far off.

The prophecy of Isaiah 14 was a prophecy against human pride. Rather than speaking of a particular ruler in history it appeared to represent the enigmatic 'king of Babylon' as symbolic of human pride, especially of those given positions of leadership and rule. Verses 12-15 are particularly important because they tell of a battle between the Creator and his creation, where the creature took his stand against the Creator and exalted himself, snatching out at being God himself.

Isaiah was clear. The creature cannot make a stand against its Creator and hope to survive. No matter how grand they seem the great ones of the earth will suffer judgment and end up in the grave just as all human beings do. Death was the punishment for the arrogance of the first human beings and it will be the end of all who act similarly (14:10-11; cf Genesis 2-3; Isaiah 2:5-22).

Of particular significance in this part of the poem was the word used for 'leaders' in Isaiah 14:9 (NIV). The word in Hebrew literally refers to a he-goat. The he-goat was the leader of the flock and hence it was used figuratively of leaders among men. Daniel also referred to a he-goat in Daniel 8:5 (although using different Hebrew words) in a context that spoke of human rulers asserting themselves against God and of God decreeing their demise.

2. The Vision (8:1-12)

(a) Susa

Daniel 8 marked a return to Hebrew from the Aramaic that had not been used since Daniel 2:4. There was a change in setting. Two years have passed and Daniel was now *in the third year of King Belshazzar's reign.* Instead of dreaming he had *a vision* (a word used to describe something that happens while you are awake, rather than when asleep) during which he found himself no longer in Babylon, but *in the citadel of Susa in the province of Elam . . beside the Ulai canal.*

Susa had been sacked by the Babylonian king Asshurbanipal, to be rebuilt by the Persian king Darius I and became a city renowned as a mighty fortress. It was the winter capital of the Persian empire, the residence of Persian kings, and therefore known in the Bible as the seat of the Persian empire (cf Esther and Nehemiah). As for the meaning of Ulai canal, it was an ancient name for a waterway near the city.

The point is that Babylon's power was declining and that the next great force on the world stage was the Persian empire, which at first glance appeared mighty and invincible. Further, the shift to Susa encourages us to relate the events depicted in the vision not to the exile but to later circumstances in history.

The vision followed the dream in chapter 7 in broad outline and was specifically linked with it in verse 1 when it was stated that it occurred *after the one that had already appeared to me.* While Chapter 7 gave a large overview which linked chapters 1-6 with larger cosmic goings on and particularly with one awesomely evil protagonist against God, chapter 8 and subsequent chapters focus on this protagonist and therefore on the nearness of the end and of judgment and vindication. For this reason Chapter 8 is more specific than chapter 7, giving a particular instance of the larger truths of chapter 7.

(b) The Ram

Verse 3 introduces us to the first of two animals that predominate the chapter, a ram and a goat. Both animals, unlike the beasts of chapter 7, are clean animals and therefore perhaps a little less terrifying or objectionable. Both are used in the Old Testament as symbols of power and therefore of leadership (cf Jeremiah 51:40; Ezekiel 34:17; 39:18; Zechariah 10:3).

There are strong similarities between the ram and the he-goat and their actions: They both appeared almost from nowhere, acted boldly and aggressively, enjoyed success, and then fell. The pattern is one that is seen in the prophets repeatedly as they talk of the rise and fall of pagan nations. God's kingship alone is lasting.

As Daniel looked he first saw *there before* him *a ram with two horns, standing beside the canal, and the horns were long.* Although there was no need of identification, the interpretation given by Gabriel in verse 20 was that this two horned ram represented *the kings of Media and Persia.* The two horns indicate that this was one united empire made up of two clearly distinguished nations. The statement *one of the horns was longer than the other but grew up later* referred to the fact that the Persian part of this kingdom arose later than that of the Medes, but exceeded it in power. Under its first great king, Cyrus, and his successors this nation extended its boundaries as it *charged toward the West and the North and the South.* No kingdom could stand against the ram and *none could rescue from his power. He did as he pleased and became great.* No one could resist his aggressive power.

(c) The He-goat

There is a famous impressionist painting of a man taking a small black dog for a walk in Paris. In an attempt to capture the movement of the dog the artist has shown the legs of the dog in a variety of different positions. The result of the portrayal is that the dog almost appears to be floating on air as it moves swiftly beside its master. Daniel's vision of a goat is somewhat similar. While Daniel pondered the significance of the ram *suddenly a goat with a prominent horn between his eyes came from the West, crossing the whole earth without touching the ground.* Like the ram before him, the speed of this goat in conquest was so profound, it was as though his feet hardly touched the ground.

Any contest between a ram and a male goat is no contest. The ferocity, superior strength, agility, and weaponry of the goat would mean that no ram could withstand an attack.

With hindsight we can identify the he-goat as the young king of Greece, Alexander the Great. The Persian empire was easily overthrown by Alexander. The he-goat attacked *the ram furiously, striking the ram and shattering its two horns. The ram was powerless to stand against him and so he is knocked . . . to the ground and trampled upon. None could rescue the ram from his power.*

The conquests of Alexander and the extent of his victories are summarised in the book of 1 Maccabees in the Old Testament apocrypha:

> Alexander of Macedon, son of Phillip, had come from the land of Kittim and defeated Darius, king of the Persians and Medes, whom he succeeded as ruler, as first of Hellas. He undertook many campaigns and gained possession of many fortresses, and put the local kings to death. So he advanced to the ends of the earth, plundering nation after nation; the earth grew silent before him, and his ambitious heart swelled with pride. He assembled very powerful forces and subdued provinces, nations and princes, and they became his tributaries. (1 Maccabees 1:1-4 [Jerusalem Bible])

Over a period of four years (334-331 BC) Alexander demolished the Persian empire and established an empire of his own extending from Europe to India. However, as with Nebuchadnezzar before him, God was able to humble those that walked in pride (Daniel 4:37), *at the height of his power* the *large horn* on the-goat's forehead was *broken off* and Alexander died (323 BC). Again, 1 Maccabees records his demise:

> But the time came when Alexander took to his bed, in the knowledge that he was dying. He summoned his comrades, noblemen who had been brought up with him from his youth, and divided his kingdom among them

while he was still alive. Alexander had reigned twelve years when he died. (1 Maccabees 1:5-7 [Jerusalem Bible])

The composite picture is striking. Although these earthly rulers were men of massive and impressive power, they were found wanting.

The conquests of Alexander in particular have changed the world. The Greek culture and learning he brought with him meant that world culture, thought, and even social structure would never be the same again. Many of these things have been tremendously positive and beneficial to our world. Nevertheless, his regime comes under God's judgment, demonstrating that the real worth of an empire is not to be measured by human standards but by whether it lives rightly under the rule of God. Alexander was no different to other rulers whether great or small. He was no different to us. And God will measure us in the same way, by how we have responded to his rule, and lived under it.

(d) *The Small Horn*

Alexander's kingdom was divided among his friends and generals, *four prominent horns* replaced the one prominent horn of Alexander. As Daniel watched out of one of the horns *came another horn, which started small but grew in power to the South and to the East and toward the Beautiful Land.* Although not named, the horn was obviously Antiochus IV. Although Alexander was an incredibly major figure in world history he figures here merely as an introduction to Antiochus, who was far more significant as far as Israelite history was concerned. Although relatively small in influence by comparison, Antiochus is as arrogant as his predecessors and some aspects excelled over them. This small horn:

- *reached the host of the heavens* and *threw some of the starry host down to earth and trampled upon them* (perhaps a reference to God's supernatural forces – cf Judges 5:20 and Job 38:7).

- *set itself up to be as great as the Prince of the host* (that is, he set himself up against God himself).

- *took away the daily sacrifice from him* (although the term daily sacrifice was often used for the whole offering sacrificed at the beginning and end of every day, it could imply the whole range of religious practices associated with the temple. Antiochus is said to have banned such a broad range of activities in 1 Maccabees 1:45).

- *brought low . . . the place of his sanctuary* (a reference to the ravaging and desecrating of the temple by Antiochus in 167 BC E cf 1 Maccabees 1:45ff).

- *prospered in everything it did* (unlike the persecutors of Daniel 1-6!).

- *caused truth to be thrown down to the ground* (Antiochus destroyed copies of the Torah and forbade the practice of various key commandments endorsed by it such as circumcision, reading it publicly, offering sacrifices, etc. – cf 1 Maccabees 1:56f).

In other words, God's army, God's sanctuary, and God's truth were thrown down by this ruler and became his victims.

There is some division amongst commentators regarding the identity of 'the host' in verse 12. The NIV here considers that 'the host' is a reference to the people of God and has therefore added the words 'of the saints' to its translation of that verse. While this interpretation is possible, the position taken here is that the host is not the host 'of the saints' but God's heavenly host, that is, his supernatural army.

3. An Interlude (8:13-14)

The noticeable feature of the description of the adventures of the small horn was that the cycle depicted for the ram and the he-goat was broken. They appeared almost from nowhere, acted boldly and aggressively, enjoyed success, and then fell. The final element in the cycle for the small horn was absent. The function of the brief interlude from verse 9-14 was to let us know that although there was no fall of the small horn all was under control. The implication is that there will be an end. This implication leads to one of the dominant issues of these verses, the question, 'How long?'. The other two issues are the rebellion which causes desolation and the 2300 days.

(a) How Long?

As Daniel watched the vision he heard a conversation that expressed the concerns he had as he watched. In his vision he heard *a holy one speaking, and another holy one said to him, 'How long will it take for the vision to be fulfilled?'* Although the holy one and Daniel are undoubtedly concerned about the inevitable persecution of the saints and its duration, the thrust of Daniel 8:13 appears to be on the assault against God himself that was being mounted by the small horn. It expressed the desire of the godly that there be an end to blasphemy and the dishonouring of God's name and glory (cf Psalm 74:10; cf Revelation 6:10). At the same time, the question represented an assertion that God was in control and that his victory was assured and only a matter of time.

(b) The Abomination of Desolation

The term *'the rebellion that causes desolation'* is important in the book as a whole. The actual Hebrew phrase used here is different to the term used in 9:27; 11:31; and 12:11 even though the same incident is being referred to. In the later verses the term used in Hebrew is *shiqquts shomem*, which appears to be a word play. Antiochus believed himself to be the earthly manifestation of the Greek god *Zeus Olympios* and it was to this god that he dedicated the Jerusalem temple when he took it over in 167 BC. We know from Josephus (*Contra Apionem* 1:17) that *Zeus Olympios* is an equivalent to the Canaanite god 'Lord of Heaven' (Hebrew, *Baal Shamem*). If the term 'Lord' (Hebrew, *Baal*, also a name of a Canaanite God) is replaced by 'rebellion' (so 8:13) or 'abomination' (Hebrew, *shiqquts* in 9:27; 11:31; 12:11) and the term 'Heaven' (Hebrew, *shamem*) is replaced by 'desolation' (Hebrew, *shomem*) we find that 'the rebellion that causes desolation' becomes a contemptuous pun.

It may very well be that Antiochus may not have understood the problem as the Jews saw it. He may not have seen that he was introducing a new god into the worship of the temple, but merely worshipping the same god under a different name. It is feasible to understand that the Greek 'Zeus Olympios' could be seen to be the equivalent of the Canaanite 'Lord of Heaven' and the Jewish 'Most High God.' Similar things had happened with other Canaanite deities such as Astarte and the like.

However, the Jews understood things very differently. They knew that God is one. They also knew that their history was littered with attempts at combining worship of the true God with the worship of the gods of the surrounding nations. For such attempts the judgment of God had been forthcoming. The Jews knew that syncretism was impossible.

Similarly we must have nothing to do with syncretism. Jesus cannot be understood under another name or superimposed on another religion. We cannot combine him with Eastern religions or mix him with New Age religion. Jesus is unique, he is the only way to God (John 14.6), and

God has given no other name by which people may be saved (Acts 4:12).

(c) 2300 Days

The holy one's question, 'how long?', was obviously Daniel's question as well since the holy one turned to him and gave the answer: *'It will take 2,300 evenings and mornings; then the sanctuary will be reconsecrated.'*

It is difficult to work out what 2,300 mornings and evenings means. Given that the Bible elsewhere uses the phrase 'evening and morning' as a way of describing one day (cf Genesis 1) perhaps we should take 2,300 mornings and evenings as 2,300 days. In this case we are dealing with a period of approximately six or seven years. While this could possibly refer to the period between the removal of Onias III as High Priest in 171 BC through to the rededication of the temple in 164, it may be better to recognise that the holy one was merely maintaining that there will be a fixed and limited time before God acts to vindicate his name and his servants and that the sign of this will be the reconsecration of the temple.

4. Rams, Goats, and Lambs

In the last two chapters of Daniel we have watched as a variety of beasts were paraded before us. Each of them represented either supernatural or human forces at work in human history. The two beasts in this chapter have been fast, strong, and vigorous. The human leaders they represented were giants in the particular era of human history from which they came.

In the book of Revelation the animal imagery is continued. There also we see dragons and various other beasts, again representing human rulers and the demonic forces behind them. Revelation also talks about Jesus using animal imagery.

It is likely that most of us, if we were asked to ascribe an animal image to Jesus would choose some animal of great magnificence or with royal connotations. Perhaps we would choose an animal such as a lion. Revelation 5 shows us that we would not be alone in looking for such an image. The Bible itself leads us to expect that the Messiah would be 'a lion from the tribe of Judah' (Genesis 49:9; Revelation 5:5). Genesis 49 links the image with rule and the overthrow of enemies.

The setting in Revelation 5 is one where a mighty angel was looking for one worthy to open a scroll which contained the story of the world's future. John was distressed because no one could be found but then is comforted by the words of one of the twenty-four elders who told him not to weep because a Lion of the tribe of Judah had triumphed and was able to open the seals. We can imagine John looking round the heavenly throne-room searching for a majestic lion with roaring mouth and free-flowing mane. As he looked no lion could be found. What he did find was a small lamb standing with blood dripping from its throat. It had the marks of being slain and yet remained still standing. With great boldness it marched to the angel and took the scroll at which point the elders fell down and worshiped and all heaven burst into songs of praise. It is not a lion who will sit on the throne of God, but a lamb.

The picture is magnificent. It shows us what the rule of God is really like. It is not rule with force of arms where subjects are beaten into unwilling submission. It is rule where the king offers himself in sacrifice for his subjects; where he comes not to be served but to serve and give his life as a ransom for many (Mark 10:45). The portrait of God's rule in action is not that of a magnificent bear, eagle, ram, goat, or lion, but of a lamb who has been willingly slain, but whom death cannot hold.

FOR STUDY, DISCUSSION AND PRAYER

1. Read Isaiah 14. What are the primary characteristics of the 'king of Babylon'? How do they compare with those of the 'small horn' in Daniel 8?

2. Give some examples of modern day syncretism (that is, the combination of Christian religion with other religions or with other religious or philosophical ideas).

3. How literally should we take the numbers of Daniel 7-12? What indications are there within the text that the numbers are to be taken literally or figuratively?

4. In using a lamb as a symbol for Jesus, what is the New Testament conveying about the way Jesus rules and carries out his ministry?

20

An End Time 'In Sight' 8:15-27

1. Gabriel (8:15-16)

The vision which Daniel saw in the first part of chapter 8 introduced us to particular figures in history. Looking back on the events of history we can identify the people that the beasts represent. This was not the case for Daniel living in the third year of King Belshazzar's reign. For him Susa was a small and as yet insignificant city and the small horn that rose from four prominent horns needed interpretation. So it was that *while* Daniel *was watching the vision and trying to understand it, there stood before* him *one who looked like a man. And* he *heard a man's voice from the Ulai calling, 'Gabriel, tell this man the meaning of the vision.'*

Upon hearing *a man's voice*, here undoubtedly a reference to the voice of God, Daniel did what is appropriate when faced with the presence of a holy one. He *was terrified and fell prostrate* at which point Gabriel spoke, fulfilling his charge and telling him *the meaning of the vision.* Verse 18 tells us that while Gabriel was speaking Daniel was in some type of trancelike sleep while still with his *face to the ground.* Then, at some point during the vision, Gabriel *touched* him and *raised* him to his feet.

2. The End (8:17-19)

Gabriel's first words to Daniel urged him to understand that the vision concerned *the time of the end*. The term 'the end' is an everyday term and does not necessarily refer to the 'End Of Time' but may refer to the end of a particular time. The same is true of the other terms regarding time (for example, *the time of wrath* in verse 19) that occur between this verse and the final verse of the chapter. An analogy from the book of Genesis might help us understand the way that these words are used here.

Genesis 1-11 is so structured as to demonstrate the nature of human sinfulness and of God's response to sin. It shows us the endemic nature of sin. All humans are sinful and every inclination of the thoughts of their hearts are continually evil (Genesis 6:5). Sin is an act of independence by the creature and as such incurs the wrath of the Creator. It deserves punishment.

Within Genesis 1-11 the flood (Genesis 6-9) was such a punishment on sin and looked like an 'end' to God's wrath. However, subsequent chapters show us that sin was far from gone in the world. The next generation were still sinful and still deserved God's wrath (cf Genesis 11). Therefore the 'end' seen in the flood was not *the* end but *an* end.

The cycle in Genesis 1-11 is obvious: God's mercy, human sinfulness, God's wrath, God's mercy (expressed in his salvation of his people such as Noah and Abraham). The very presence of this cycle indicates that it will be a facet of every age and that there will be a final 'end' when God finally acts to bring wrath on evildoers and salvation to his people.

If we apply this principle to Daniel it helps us understand the thought of the book. The exile and return looked like *the* end of God's wrath (cf Isaiah 40:1-2), but were in fact *an* end and therefore only symbols of *the* end. This point is developed more fully in chapter 9.

However, Daniel was going further than this. The presence of chapter 7 and the language of chapters 8-12 suggested that not even the end of the tyrant Antiochus is *the* end, but also merely *an* end symbolic of *the* end. This is supported by the fact that where Daniel 7 gave no specific identification of the beasts and horns, chapter 8 did. In other words, Chapter 7 was the broad canvas, showing the broad principles and chapter 8 was but one example in history of these forces at work.

3. Interpreting Daniel's Vision (8:20-25)

(a) Naming the Beasts

As we noted earlier, the identification of *the two horned ram* with *the kings of Media and Persia, the shaggy goat with the king of Greece*, and *the large horn with the first king* of Greece was scarcely needed, being obvious from the start of the vision. The implication of the naming of the beasts was that these specific kings represent trans historical, supernatural forces.

So too, the reference to the *four horns that replaced the one that was broken off* and their representing *four kingdoms that will emerge from his nation but will not have the same power* is easily understood. It is as a reference to the Diadochi who continued Alexander's rule, though not as successfully as he. Similarly, the *stern faced king* who was to follow them refers obviously to Antiochus Epiphanes. However, the gradual shift away from identification (Greece and Persia) and towards ambiguity is noticeable and performs an important function. It highlights that although we are dealing with specific historical circumstances there are larger supernatural forces operating behind the human figure of Antiochus. There is a battle going on that is both timeless and operating on a much larger scale than one petty tyrant in the second century BC.

(b) The Tyrant

The king of verses 23-25, that is depicted as assuming power will have the standard marks of a tyrant. He will be bold (he will be *stern-faced* and one who *will consider himself superior*, taking *his stand against the Prince of princes*); powerful (*he will become very strong*); ruthless (*he will destroy the mighty men and the holy people*); clever (*a master of intrigue*); and one who *will cause deceit to prosper*. As we saw in verse 11 his stand against the Prince of princes (or 'leader of leaders') will be a stand against God himself.

The words *'but not by his own power'* are the same Hebrew words as those at the end of verse 22 and probably mean the same thing (that is, *'but will not have the same power'*). Their import was that Antiochus was strong, but not as strong as his predecessor. Some of the Greek translations of Daniel omit this reference to power altogether.

When verse 25 says that this tyrant will *be destroyed, but not by human power* (RSV *by no human hand*) we are reminded of Daniel 2:34 and 45 where the statue on the plain is destroyed by a rock carved from a mountain *not by human hands*. The point is that however this man falls, as eventually he must, his fall will be the result of divine intervention (even if it involves the use of human agents). His fall will come about because God will decide to make an end to his reign, just as he did with Nebuchadnezzar through Cyrus.

4. Facing the Truth (8:26-27)

Gabriel's assurance regarding *the vision of the evenings and mornings* given to Daniel was that it was not an illusion but true and reliable. Given the prophecies of Isaiah and the imminence of the reign of Cyrus, the temptation to think of the restoration of the temple as taking place in the imminent future would have been strong. Such a hope would be reinforced by the view that prophecy was normally thought to address current situations, not far distant ones. For this reason Daniel was told that the vision *concerns the distant future* and he was instructed to *seal up the vision.*

Daniel's problem was now severe. He knew the future. This knowledge was, on the one hand comforting, because it told him that God was in control and would eventually triumph. On the other hand, this knowledge was troubling and *appalling* because, although it spoke of events *beyond understanding* in detail, the general thrust was that the future for the people of God and the prospects of God being given his rightful honour were disturbingly grim. However, although *exhausted and ill for several days*, he knew that he had to get on with life in the world of the present. The present posed enough of its own problems and he had a king both in heaven and on earth that he must serve. Therefore Daniel *got up and went about the king's business.*

5. A Pattern For the Future

(a) Isaiah 14

We began our study of Daniel 8 by looking at Isaiah 14. While we rightly have cautions about the Christian and Jewish mythology that associates the figure in Isaiah 14 with Satan and his fall, the Bible does show a development of ideas through this chapter. The figure in Isaiah 14 (perhaps drawing on older mythical figures) was a human figure who vaunted himself against God, seeking to take God's place.

As we have seen, Daniel draws on this image regarding Antiochus and Antiochus himself in turn becomes the symbol for all human rule that similarly lifts itself up against God. The New Testament takes up this symbol and in turn uses it within its own apocalyptic literature. The actions of this small horn, which have Satanic forces behind them, become the actions of a figure in the New Testament who although known by a variety of names, is best know as the 'Antichrist'.

In 2 Thessalonians Paul talks of a day of vindication and salvation for the people of God and notes that it will not happen until 'the rebellion occurs and the man of lawlessness is revealed.' This human figure will 'oppose and will exalt himself over everything that is called God or is worshipped, so that he sets himself up in God's temple, proclaiming himself to be God' (perhaps a reference in the first instance to Caligula's decree of 40 AD that a statue of himself be erected inside the Temple). His coming will be 'in accordance with the work of Satan' and will be ended by the coming of Jesus (2 Thessalonians 2:1-12).

Similarly the book of Revelation talks of Satan (the dragon of Revelation 12) who waged war in heaven against God and his host. This dragon gave his power to an earthly counterpart (the beast of Revelation 13) who waged war against the people of God and who lifted himself up against God himself.

The important point made here is that in our world there are satanic forces at work behind the scenes (Paul's 'principalities and powers'). The influence of such powers can be seen in the rule of individual tyrants, but also in ideas, institutions, and nations that think they can replace God and treat him with contempt. It is right that we as Christians should seek to recognise such forces, not by adding up numbers in names or making speculative calculations based on Scripture, but by noticing their characteristics. It is also right that Christians should seek to oppose such people and institutions through their prayers and actions, recognising that although their fall will surely happen, it will happen only when God so ordains. Such powers will fall not by human hands, but because of the victory won over Satan through the cross of Christ.

What we have seen in chapter 8 of Daniel is a development of Isaiah 14. There we saw a specific instance of a human king rising up against God and seeking to usurp God's place. Daniel 8 has given us an instance of this and told us that there will come a point in history where a specific king will set himself against God. Symbolic of this will be his taking over of the temple and his attempt to supplant worship of the true God with worship of himself and his false God. What happens in Daniel 8 and with Antiochus Epiphanes is not new. It is part of the way the world runs and the way human kings and human agencies operate. It is not surprising therefore that Jesus prophesied that such would be part of the end times (Mark 13). We who read Daniel 8 now and who understand the person and work of Christ can also draw comfort from the implication of the chapter, that the 'end' of Antiochus and those who mould themselves after him testifies to the final end of those who lie behind them. Like the king of Babylon they will be brought down to the grave, the depths of the pit (Isaiah 14:15).

FOR STUDY, DISCUSSION AND PRAYER

1. What does 'the end' refer to in Daniel 8?

2. Read 2 Thessalonians 2:1-12 and Revelation 13. What are the characteristic attitudes and actions of (1) the man of lawlessness, and (2) the beast?

3. How appropriate is it to identify a particular person in history (for example, Hitler) with the beast in Revelation 13 or the man of lawlessness in 2 Thessalonians?

4. How does Isaiah 14 and Daniel 8 help us to understand and cope with rulers in our world who have become tyrants? What is the Christian response to their tyrannical rule?

21

How Long, O Lord?
9:1-14

1. The Question Of The Godly

The people of God are those who have lined themselves up with God and with his purposes for his world. They have experienced his mercy and accepted his redemption. They know that his purposes are always good and that he always has the best interests of his people in mind. Therefore they long for his purposes to be fulfilled and are assured that they will be fulfilled.

Because the people of God have lined themselves up with God and his purposes they are also aware that most of the world is in opposition. Their fellow humans are set against God, doubting his benevolence, opposing his grace, and resisting his rule. The people of God know that the world is also opposed to them for they act and speak in such a way as to remind people of God's rule.

For these reasons the godly have a persistent question at the forefront of their minds: 'How long?' (cf Revelation 6:10). The question comes in many forms. How long will particular evil persons last and how long will all godless powers last? How long before justice prevails? How long before God asserts himself against his opposition? How long before God acts to restore his honour, to hallow his name (Matthew

6:9-10), and to save and redeem his people? How long before usurpers to God's kingship are thrown down as they inevitably must be (Daniel 2)?

Daniel overheard *a holy one* asking , *'How long will it take for the vision to be fulfilled?'* From Daniel's conduct in the second half of chapter 8 and his deep distress over the vision, it appeared as though this question also became Daniel's question. He was concerned for the future and for the people of God who would suffer in that future. So aligned with God's purpose was he, so in tune with the future of the people of God, that it was as though he himself were there asking the question.

Since no answer was forthcoming Daniel rallied and decided that life would have to go on without an answer. *He got up* and continued to live before God in the service of the king. *He went about the king's business.* And so he continued until the reign of Darius, serving a human king, but serving a greater King as well. He remained concerned for the King of heaven's glory and honour and prayerful about the people of the King of heaven and their future.

2. Starting On An Answer

(a) The Place To Go For Answers

Perhaps it was in this frame of mind, with the question of 'How long?' on his mind, that he found himself pondering the Scriptures *in the first year of Darius son of Xerxes*. He knew that through reading and constant study of them he would find out the purposes of God and his means of working in his world. Ultimately the answers he wanted would be there and the more he studied, the more likely he would be to find answers.

However, he also knew that the Scriptures could never be interpreted in a vacuum. To interpret them rightly he would need enlightenment. This was especially so when he discovered yet again the words of Jeremiah that *the desolation of Jerusalem would last seventy years.* Somehow he knew that they held the key to the issue of time. Somehow they were linked in with the question of 'How long?' He read the passages again, thinking about them, tossing them over and over again in his mind, praying over them, seeking God's enlightenment and revelation. With the Scriptures before him, he *turned to the Lord God and pleaded with him in prayer and petition, in fasting, and in sackcloth and ashes.*

The words Daniel read were these:

Therefore the Lord Almighty says this: 'Because you have not listened to my words, I will summon all the peoples of the North and my servant Nebuchadnezzar king of Babylon,' declares the Lord, 'and I will bring them against this land and its inhabitants and against all the surrounding nations. I will completely destroy them and make them an object of horror and scorn, and an everlasting ruin. I will banish from them the sounds of joy and gladness, the voices of bride and bridegroom, the sound of millstones and the light of the lamp. This whole country will become a desolate wasteland, and these nations will serve the king of Babylon for seventy years.' (Jeremiah 25:8-11)

This is what the Lord says, 'When seventy years are completed for Babylon, I will come to you and fulfil my gracious promise to bring you back to this place. For I know the plans I have for you,' declares the Lord, 'plans to prosper you and not to harm you, plans to give you hope and a future. Then you will call upon me and come and pray to me, and I will listen to you. You will seek me and find me when you seek me with all your heart. I will be found by you,' declares the Lord, 'and will bring you back from captivity.' (Jeremiah 29:10-14)

It seems as though Daniel was especially struck by the words

'Then you will call upon me and come and pray to me, and I will listen to you. You will seek me and find me when you seek me with all your heart. I will be found by you,' declares the Lord, 'and will bring you back from captivity.' (Jeremiah 29:12)

There he was, sitting in exile as Jeremiah had prophesied, reading about Jeremiah's seventy years. The words had come to him with the force of the Spirit, 'I will restore you when you seek me and pray.' Forgetting about the end and the question of, 'how long?', he began to pray. He realised that Jeremiah had the correct perspective, the secret of this difficulty was found in prayer.

(b) The Problem With Darius

Before looking in detail at the prayer it is important to note the problems raised concerning verse 1. In this verse we are told a number of things about Darius:

- He was *the son of Xerxes.*
- He was *a Mede by descent.*
- He was *made ruler of the Babylonian kingdom.*

Although, at first glance, these ascriptions would seem to question the identification of Darius with Cyrus (cf 5:31), detailed analysis does not prohibit this identification (see the discussion of the issue in commentaries by Baldwin and Goldingay). In fact, the identification of Darius with Cyrus is helpful in understanding the setting of the prayer of Daniel. The prophet Isaiah had indicated that the ascension of Cyrus would mark a new phase in Israelite history. He would be God's anointed one (Hebrew 'Messiah;' Greek 'Christ' – cf Isaiah 45:1) who would return the exiles to their own land (Isaiah 45:13). The first year of the reign of Cyrus would therefore be an appropriate time to be meditating on the prophecies of Jeremiah that spoke of the end of the exile. It was the right time for seeking God in prayer.

3. The Prayer Of Daniel

(a) Its Components: Confession And Supplication

Daniel's prayer is one of the great prayers of the Bible. It is made up of two major components, confession and supplication, both of which were demanded by the prophet Jeremiah.

Confession was necessary because of the sin that had been committed. Seventy years of exile had been prophesied because the Israelites had closed their ears to God for so long, rejecting him, the true God, and rebelling against his just and merciful rule.

After confession Daniel turned to *prayer and petition,* pleading with God and requesting that he forgive and rescue the Israelites.

(b) Daniel's Attitude in Praying

(i) With seriousness

Daniel threw his whole being into the exercise of prayer. His prayer was not a half muttered few words before resuming duties in the court, but something done with seriousness, with *fasting, and in sackcloth and ashes.* He said,

'O Lord, the great and awesome God who keeps his covenant of love with all those who love him and obey his commands, we have sinned and done wrong. We have been wicked and have rebelled; we have turned away from your commands and laws. We have not listened to your servants the prophets, who spoke in your name to our kings, our princes, our fathers, and to all the people of the land.'

(ii) In a solidarity of sinfulness

The striking thing about the prayer is the word '*we*'. Daniel does not say, '*They* sinned, and now *we* are reaping the consequences,' but '*we* have sinned. *We* have done wrong. *We* have acted wickedly. *We* have rebelled. *We* have not listened to your servants the prophets.'

The same emphasis continues throughout the prayer.

'O Lord, we and our kings, our princes and our fathers are covered with shame because we have sinned against you . . . we have rebelled against him, we have not obeyed . . . we have sinned against you . . . we have not sought the favour of the Lord our God by turning from our sins and giving attention to your truth . . . we have not obeyed him . . . we have sinned, we have done wrong.'

Daniel was doing three things here. First, he was identifying himself with the sin of his ancestors. It was not only a group of *kings* and *princes* who sinned. Nor was it just the fathers of the nation. Rather, it was *all Israel* who sinned. God had spoken through his prophets not only to *kings* and *princes* and to the *fathers*, but also *to all the people of the land* (verse 6). It was *all Israel* who *transgressed* God's *law and turned away, refusing to obey him* (verse 11).

Furthermore, the sin committed was culpable. It was not as though Israel was not in a relationship with God or had not known God and his commandments. By talking about God in personal terms (*your commands . . . your prophets . . .*) Daniel acknowledged the personal relationship existing between God and the nation. There was a covenant between them. That relationship had guidelines for a correct response. It had *commands and laws*. Moreover, God had sent his *servants the prophets* to speak further in his name, but the people had *turned away from the commands and laws* and had *not listened* to his *servants the prophets*. The sin committed had been active and was culpable.

Daniel's prayer is a reminder to us. Because we are his creation, we are in relationship with him. However, we have ignored him and acted independently of him. We too are not without sin and our forefather Adam is not on his own in his rebellion. We follow him and belong to him. Sin characterises our relationship with God as well and therefore we cannot be the first to throw the stone at other sinners (cf Romans 5:12-21).

(iii) On behalf of others

Secondly, Daniel prayed on behalf of others. It was the prayer of one who acted as a representative of the nation, praying for his own sinfulness and for theirs. He represented them before God.

The New Testament also knows of this type of prayer and this type of faith. It was the faith of the group (perhaps as well as the faith of the man himself) who lowered their paralytic friend through the roof in Mark 3 which brought forgiveness of sin. So also 1 John 5:16 reminds us that if we see a brother commit a sin that does not lead to death, we can pray for him and that God will forgive and give life. Similarly, when we have a church which is lukewarm, we can pray on its behalf and ask Jesus to visit and give life (Revelation 3:2). The prayer of a righteous person on behalf of others is powerful and effective, bringing forgiveness and healing (James 5:13-18).

(iv) On the basis of God's promises

Thirdly, Daniel was urging God to forgive on the basis of his promises. He was doing what the people of God regularly do. He was reminding himself of the character, promises and purposes of God as revealed in his word and urging him to act on behalf of them. Some of the Scriptures which lie behind his prayer are those found in 1 Kings 8 (cf 2 Chronicles 6), Jeremiah 26, 32 and 44. Perhaps most significant is the prayer recorded in 1 Kings 8.

When they sin against you – for there is no one who does not sin – and you become angry with them and give them over to the enemy, who takes them captive to his own land, far away or near; and if they have a change of heart in the land where they are held captive, and repent and plead with you in the land of their conquerors and say, 'We have sinned, we have done wrong, we have acted wickedly'; and if they turn back to you with all their heart and soul in the land of their enemies who took them captive, and pray to you towards the land you gave to their fathers, towards the city you have chosen and the temple I have built for your Name; then from heaven, your dwelling-place, hear their prayer and their plea, and uphold their cause. And forgive your people, who have sinned against you; forgive all the offences they have committed against you, and cause their conquerors to show them mercy; for they are your people and your inheritance, whom you brought out of Egypt, out of that iron-smelting furnace. May your eyes be open to your servant's plea and to the plea of your people Israel, and may you listen to them whenever they cry out to you. For you singled them out from all the

nations of the world to be your own inheritance, just as
you declared through your servant Moses when you, O
Sovereign Lord, brought our fathers out of Egypt.'
(1 Kings 8:46-53)

We too can do what Daniel did.   We can read the
Scriptures to understand the character of God and become
aware of his promises and purposes in the world. We can pray
urging him to act according to them.   In essence this is what
Jesus did in the Lord's Prayer. These are the prayers which
are assured of eventual success; prayers which are according
to his will and therefore ones we can be sure he will hear and
answer (cf 1 John 5:14-15).

(v)   Acknowledging God's righteousness

In verse 7 Daniel affirmed and acknowledged, *'Lord, you
are righteous'*.   In effect, he was saying: 'Lord, you are right,
we belong here in exile.   This is where we should be given
your kingly rule and your covenant with us.   We are where
we deserve to be given your righteousness, holiness, justice,
and kingly rule.'
The blame for the situation that Israel found itself in can
only be placed fairly upon the nation itself.   God is blameless.
It is this assertion that provides the basis for the next section
of the prayer.

FOR STUDY, DISCUSSION AND PRAYER

1. Read the Lord's Prayer in Matthew 6:9-13. In the light of Daniel, what is the meaning of the requests in verses 9-10?

2. Summarise what Daniel 9 teaches about prayer.

3. Read James 5:13-18 and 1 John 5:13-17. In what ways is the content of these passages similar to that of Daniel 9?

4. Spend some time praying for yourself and your own Christian community along the lines suggested by Daniel 9.

22

Living With God's Answer 9:15-27

1. The Basis of An Appeal to God

(a) His Nature to Have Mercy

Verses 15 and 16 are a high point in Daniel's prayer. In these verses he cast himself on the nature and character of God as he was known in his kingly rule, in his nature to have mercy.

> 'Now, O Lord our God, who brought your people out of Egypt with a mighty hand and who made for yourself a name that endures to this day, we have sinned, we have done wrong. O Lord, in keeping with your righteous acts, turn away your anger and your wrath from Jerusalem, your city, your holy hill. Our sins and the iniquities of our fathers have made Jerusalem and your people an object of scorn to all those around us.'

Daniel demonstrated a very important principle which arose from his reading of the Scriptures. He did not say, 'Turn away your anger and your wrath because we have now improved. We have got better, sinned less, rebelled less furiously.' Nor did he say, 'Turn away your anger and your wrath because we are now without sin' or 'Turn away your anger and your wrath because now I, Daniel, am a holy and godly man, unlike all my ancestors.' Instead he said, 'God, we still deserve your wrath and anger, but please be merciful, please turn away your anger and your wrath from our sin.' The first ground for God's activity is not found outside him, but within, in his own being, in his nature to have mercy.

(b) His Glory

Daniel then appealed to the second ground for God's redemptive activity towards his people, his own glory.

> *'Now, our God, hear the prayers and petitions of your servant. For your sake, O Lord, look with favour on your desolate sanctuary.'*

In other words, Daniel urged God to act for his own sake. He was saying, 'God, it is your city that has been devastated, it is your people who are an object of scorn, it is against you that the nations are setting themselves. For your sake turn things around, for your sake restore Jerusalem.'

> *'Give ear, O God, and hear! Open your eyes and see the desolation of the city that bears your name. We do not make requests of you on the basis of our own righteousness, but on the basis of your great mercy. O Lord, listen! O Lord, forgive! O Lord, hear and act! For your sake, O my God, do not delay, because your city and your people bear your name.'*

This is a clear insight into the character of Daniel. The Daniel who stood against Nebuchadnezzar and the great kings of the Ancient Near East was utterly dependent upon God. He knew that all that he had and all that he was came from God. Any mercy he received, any rescue he experienced, any righteousness he had, was the gift of God.

Daniel was a man who knew about and lived in the grace of God. Therefore as he read Jeremiah, looking at his own sin and the sin of his own generation, and the sin of previous generations, he did what he had always done. He cast himself upon the mercy and grace of God. There was nothing in him or his people that deserved a response from God, but it is God's nature to care for his own. Daniel knew that the King of heaven was a King who ruled with compassion and kindness, who was loyal to his covenant and faithful to his word. He knew that he could rely on this when he could rely on nothing else.

It is these truths that provide our ultimate ground of assurance. They are the prerequisites for a relationship with God and for experience of his salvation and redemption. To be saved and to continue to live in the presence of God we must rely on these truths about God. We must believe that he is and that it is his nature to be merciful. We must be convicted of our own sin and convinced that he will act as he has promised, that he will judge the guilty and forgive the repentant. All we can do is cling to his mercy, fully and finally demonstrated in the cross of Christ. All who grasp these truths about God and call upon him will be saved. It is his nature to have mercy and to save. He cannot be God if he does not act like this.

2. The God Who Acts

While Daniel *was speaking and praying* and *confessing* his sins and the sins of his people, and urging God to respond, God was already active. *While* the words were still on his lips God answered by sending *Gabriel, the man* he had *seen in the earlier vision,* who came to him *in swift flight.*

So it always is with God. He is only too ready to listen to the prayers of his saints, eager to respond as they call upon his character and seek to honour his name. Answers fly quickly from a God such as this.

From God, Gabriel arrived with an explanation, stressing God's readiness to answer Daniel's prayer: *'Daniel, I have now come to give you insight and understanding. As soon as you began to pray, an answer was given, which I have come to tell you, for you are highly esteemed. Therefore, consider the message and understand the vision.'*

The words of Gabriel were strange because they spoke about a 'vision.' However, fear and confusion about the vision was not the immediate problem. There had been no vision of recent times about which Daniel had been concerned. His concerns had been more with the exile and its end.

Gabriel's words told Daniel that the two were linked. Daniel was worried and appalled about the vision in chapter 8 because it showed an evil power exerting itself against God and against his people. He was also worried about the situation in the exile because it was a situation in which God was being mocked and scorned and his people were away from their land and their city Jerusalem. What is happening in these verses is that Gabriel was reinterpreting Jeremiah for Daniel, pointing out that if Daniel was really interested in God's purposes in history then he needed to look beyond the exile and think beyond seventy weeks. He needed to think in terms of seven times seventy.

> *Seventy weeks of years are decreed for the people of God and for the holy city to finish transgression, to put an end to sin, to atone for wickedness, to bring in everlasting righteousness, to seal up the vision and prophecy and to anoint the most holy.*

This is where God is leading his people. This is his goal for their history. God's mercy and his concern for his honour will reach a climax when:

- transgression has finished;
- sin has been put to an end;
- iniquity has been atoned for;
- everlasting righteousness has been brought in;
- the vision of Daniel and the dream of Jeremiah have been sealed (fulfilled); and
- a most holy has been anointed.

3. What Does This All Mean?

There can be no doubt that these verses found their first fulfilment in the events of the second century when God acted to save his people from a particularly aggressive and vindictive oppressor, Antiochus Epiphanes. However, like Daniel and Gabriel, we need to be wise about interpreting this passage. Together these two figures showed us a way to decipher their message.

(a) Daniel's Approach to Interpreting Jeremiah

Consider Daniel's approach. He started with questions about the future and about his own day. He then searched the Scriptures in order to find answers. He found Jeremiah and then Gabriel showed him that the prophecy of Jeremiah demonstrated a pattern in the way God acted in his world. The pattern went something like this.

- Israel sinned against God year after year after year.
- Under the hand of God, Nebuchadnezzar lifted himself against God.
- He acted brutally against God's people and was God's instrument to punish them.

- However, he had only been allowed to do this for a limited time. After seventy years sin would be atoned for.
- At the right time then, God acted and Nebuchadnezzar and his kingdom had gone the way of all the kingdoms of men.
- The instrument for this was God's anointed one, Cyrus.

So it would be in the future (see chapter 8).

- A king would lift himself up against God (8:9-11).
- He would brutalise the people of God (8:10b-12, 24-25).
- But he would only be allowed to do this for a limited time (8:14).
- And after this God would act and bring down this kingdom of man just as he brings down all kingdoms of men (8:25b).

God's goal in all of this was to bring in a situation where:

- transgression has finished;
- sin has been put to an end;
- iniquity has been atoned for;
- everlasting righteousness has been brought in;
- the vision of Daniel and the dream of Jeremiah have been sealed (fulfilled); and
- a most holy has been anointed.

This is the pattern of God's activity and the goal of his activity in his world.

Christians know that there is only one place in history where these things have happened in a lasting, complete, and indisputable way. Only in the person of Jesus are these things finally fulfilled. In Jesus the pattern laid down in Jeremiah and Daniel finally reached its climax. He is God's 'Yes' to all his promises (2 Corinthians 1:20).

Gabriel's point was that there will be a completeness of years, a seventy times seven completeness. At this time God will act in history. He will fulfil his purposes and the goal of his kingly rule will be realised and fulfilled. As Christians we know its end. It is the person and work of Jesus, the Anointed One.

4. 'How Long, O Lord?'

The next few verses are notoriously difficult ones. Gabriel told Daniel to *'Know and understand this: From the issuing of the decree to restore and rebuild Jerusalem until the Anointed One, the ruler, comes, there will be seven 'sevens', and sixty-two 'sevens'. It will be rebuilt with streets and a trench, but in times of trouble. After the sixty-two 'sevens', the Anointed One will be cut off and will have nothing. The people of the ruler who will come will destroy the city and the sanctuary. The end will come like a flood. War will continue until the end, and desolations have been decreed. He will confirm a covenant with many for one 'seven'. In the middle of the 'seven' he will put an end to sacrifice and offering. And on a wing of the temple, he will set up an abomination that causes desolation, until the end that is decreed is poured out on him.'*

(a) The Fundamental Point

Although you can add up the numbers and align them with bits of second century Jewish history this is not the fundamental point of the passage. It is found by looking at the verses in the total context of the chapter.

Verse 24, for example, is related to the first half of Daniel's prayer and is designed to answer it. He had spent his time confessing sin and acknowledging the people's need for forgiveness. He was, in effect, asking God about sin. Verse

24 is the answer to this question. It says, 'It will be done away with. There will be an end to it and to the punishment which follows it.'

The second half of Daniel's prayer had a different focus and in it he posed a different question. The question put to God there was about God restoring his position. In verse 25 God answered this question. His answer can be summarised in the following manner:

'Daniel, I will restore it. It is determined. The end of desolations will indeed be an end. Accept and understand that I am in control of time and times. There will be a time and there will be periods of time. Various historical things will happen, but in the long run, Daniel, you can be assured that I am in control and that an end time is predetermined. Even more, be assured that an end of desolation and sacrilege is predetermined. It will happen. Be assured, Daniel, I will not delay and I will answer your prayer. I will cause my name and my people who are called by my name to be vindicated.'

God is not asking Daniel to play number games with him, but begging him to understand his control. He is behind the processes of history and will bring answers to the prayers of Daniel. He will come speedily and not delay in answering the prayers of all those who long for forgiveness, justice, and an end to the dishonouring of God and the persecution of his people. He will be merciful and he will act on behalf of his name and his people.

5. Living With The Promises

Gabriel's revelation must have been particularly difficult for Daniel. All his life he and his fellow Jews had waited for Nebuchadnezzar to be brought to an end by God. All his life he had lived with his own sin and the sin of his parents. He longed for the day of forgiveness and atonement and the termination of the exile.

With the end of Belshazzar and the beginning of the reign of the Medes and Persians under Cyrus and his policies he saw a light at the end of the tunnel. Before long the return would begin. There would be a new exodus and entry into the land, to Jerusalem, and perhaps even a new temple. With this new day there were chances of a new beginning.

Yet, as he prayed, God let him know that although there might be a return to the land and to Jerusalem, his purposes would not be finally realised there. There was still a long way to go. These days were not the days of salvation. They were not the day of the Lord that so many had hoped for. That day was coming, but it was coming in the future.

And so it was that Daniel lived. He dreamt more, he experienced more, he lived on in Babylon while many of his fellow Jews journeyed back to the pile of rubble that had once been Jerusalem. Eventually he died without the answers to his prayers being realised in history. He did not witness the promised victory of God and the end of kingdoms opposed to God. Nor did he see the end of the persecution of the people of God. On the contrary, his dreams revealed that the persecution of the people would increase and grow.

The man who had spent most of his long life representing God in a pagan court died with his greatest yearnings unfulfilled, without having seen Jerusalem, and looking for some future day. Like so many, he was still living in hope and faith when he died. He did not receive the things promised and dreamt about. He watched for them and welcomed them from a distance, recognising that he was an alien and stranger in the courts of Babylon and even on earth itself. He was from another city, another country, and to this city he looked daily, praying towards the symbol of its existence, a pile of rubble on a hill to the West, named Jerusalem.

It is from the mouths of such people as Daniel that God loves to hear his name pronounced. He is not ashamed to be called the God of such people, and for them he has prepared a better city (cf Hebrews 11:13-15). The principles Daniel worked out in Babylon and the dreams he had dreamt, were not only of significance for his age, but also for ages to come. They spoke of eternal principles for God's people in every age.

How many of us are like Daniel? How many of us will continue with our prayers in the way Daniel did? How many will pray to God, accepting that he has his own purpose in mind, and leave it with him? How many of us will be willing to not see the answers to our prayers and still believe in the God of history?

Only the person of faith can do this. That is the point of Hebrews 11. Daniel did not receive what was promised. His heartfelt prayers were not answered in his own lifetime. He had not seen the day when transgression was finished and all the other promises fulfilled. Nevertheless, he put his faith and his trust in God, becoming a model for all those who are required to do the same thing in light of the same difficulties. These are those who seal the mouths of lions. These are those by whom God is not ashamed to be called God.

FOR STUDY, DISCUSSION AND PRAYER

1. In what sense can Daniel 9 be seen as an answer to prayer? Is it an answer that would satisfy you? If not, why not?

2. On what basis does Daniel appeal to God? Can we do the same? If so, then give some New Testament examples of such prayers as well as some you might pray in your own situation.

3. What have you learnt about the character of God and the godly person through examining Daniel's prayer?

23

A Heavenly Messenger 10:1-11:1

1. The Third Year Of Cyrus (1:1)

Chapters 10-12 belong together and concern one revelation given to Daniel. It is the longest single section within the whole book and although it has points of contact with each of chapters 7, 8, and 9, its detail and presentation most closely corresponds to chapter 8. Nearly every verse of chapter 8 reappears in identical or similar guise within the introduction and the revelation proper.

There are three major sections to this part of the book:

10:1-11:1   An introduction to the vision proper.

11:2-39   A description of four kingdoms, with a focus on the fourth.

11:40-12:4   A prediction concerning the 'end time.'

12:5-13   A conclusion to the section, and to the book as a whole.

The introduction has a number of important elements:

- It gives the setting: the third year of Cyrus, king of Persia. That is, well after the decree to restore the temple and to allow any Israelites who wished to undertake the task of restoration to return to Jerusalem.

- It concerns a 'revelation'. (It is similar in style to Daniel 9 rather than 7 or 8).

- It came to Daniel who was also known as Belteshazzar. (This name had previously only been used in chapters 1 - 6, thus a link is forged between this chapter and the earlier chapters).

- Its message is *true*, that is, it is trustworthy and reliable, and understanding of its message is communicated in a vision. (This comment forges a link between previous chapters concerning dreams and visions, but particularly chapter 8).

- It concerns *a great war*. (This in itself is striking since Isaiah 40:1-2, addressed to the Israelites at a similar time talks about Israel's warfare having ended. Again, we are being told that the end of the exile is not a final end to Israel's tribulation. There is more to come).

2. Beside the River Tigris (10:2-15)

(a) Mourning

It is this last point that may explain the reference to the fact that Daniel *mourned for three weeks*. On the other hand, it could be that the mourning could merely be his way of preparing for the receiving of a revelation. In any case, he engaged in practices suitable for mourning. He *ate no choice food* and *no meat or wine touched his lips*. He did not *use lotions at all until the three weeks were over* (that is, he did not anoint himself with oils, which appears to have been a normal part of daily personal grooming and a sign of health and well being – cf 2 Samuel 12:20; 14:2; Amos 6:6).

Then, *on the twenty fourth day of the first month* he looked up and *saw a man dressed in linen, with a belt of the finest gold around his waist. His body was like chrysolite, his face like lightning, his eyes like the gleam of burnished bronze, and his voice like the sound of a multitude.*

This vision took place while Daniel was *standing on the bank of the great river, the Tigris* in the company of other people. Although Daniel alone *saw the vision*, the others were *overwhelmed* with *terror* and *fled and hid themselves*. With their flight Daniel was left *gazing* at the *vision*. He too became greatly distressed; his *strength* vanished; his *face turned deathly pale*, and he became *helpless*.

(b) Revelation

We are not told who this man dressed in linen was, but he appeared to be an angelic figure. He was not God in that he was *sent* by someone else and brought a message (verse 11). Upon seeing this majestic figure and hearing *him speaking*, Daniel reacted similarly to the way he had in chapter 8. He *fell into a deep sleep*, his *face to the ground*. As in chapter 8, *a hand touched* him and set him *trembling* on his *hands and knees* (cf Daniel 8:18). His message to Daniel was that he was one *highly esteemed* by God, a man to whom God looked, and one to whom God was about to give a special revelation. At the messenger's suggestion, Daniel *stood up*, albeit *trembling*.

With Daniel standing, the messenger *continued*, telling Daniel that *since the first day that* he *had set* his mind *to gain understanding and to humble* himself before God, his words had been heard. As we saw in chapter 9 and in chapter 2, God's eyes are on the faithful who seek him in prayer and he is speedy in answering their prayers (cf Luke 18:6-8). At the beginning of the three weeks the messenger set out *in response* to Daniel's prayers. Nevertheless, there had been a delay in getting to Daniel. The delay had been caused by *the prince of the Persian kingdom* who had *resisted* the messenger *for twenty-one days* (that is, three weeks). This 'prince of the Persian kingdom' is a reference to an angelic or supernatural figure who represented the Persian kingdom before God. *Because he was detained* from coming, *Michael, one of the chief princes* came to help, taking up the battle and thus allowing the messenger to *come to explain* to Daniel *what will happen to* his *people in the future*.

(c) Spiritual Forces in the Heavenly Places

In 2 Kings 6:8ff there is a story about Elisha which helps us understand what is happening in these verses of Daniel referring to angelic beings. There we are told that the king of Aram was at war with Israel, and that his efforts were being hampered by Elisha's ability to know his troop movements and therefore inform the Israelite king and army where they should be on guard. On hearing of Elisha's actions the king of Aram sent his troops to capture Elisha. In the middle of the night, they surrounded the city where he was staying so that when Elisha and his servant rose at daybreak they found themselves encircled. Elisha's servant was petrified. Elisha prayed that God might open his eyes so that he might see the real state of things. In answer to his prayer the servant looked and saw the hills around Elisha full of horses and chariots of fire. Behind this man of God stood angelic forces which assembled to protect him and do battle on his behalf.

Elsewhere in the Old Testament we have glimpses that such forces not only are arrayed behind godly individuals, but also the nation as a whole. God was on the side of his people and did battle on their behalf, often through supernatural beings (cf Exodus 15:3ff; Deuteronomy 33:1-2;

Judges 5:19-20; 2 Samuel 5:22-24). Behind Israel and her armies lie the armies of God. Yahweh is a man of war. He is the Lord of hosts.

There are further references to supernatural beings in other Old Testament passages. Ezekiel 28, in talking of the prince of Tyre, may mean a specific angelic being representing Tyre who set himself against God. Passages like Isaiah 24:21 speak of supernatural beings who have opposed God.

The book of Daniel builds on such ideas. We find the idea of nations being represented by 'patron angels' who supported the cause of their nations (cf Deuteronomy 32:8-9). The prince of the Persian kingdom, for example, perhaps disliking the mission of the messenger and opposing his revelation concerning the vindication of Israel, resisted him coming to Daniel.

Such ideas and language in turn help us understand some important ideas in the New Testament. The Hebrew word 'prince' used in Daniel is translated in the Greek version of the Old Testament by the same word which is then used in all four of the Gospels and in Paul's writings to describe Satan or evil spirit powers (for example, Matthew 9:34; 12:24; John 12:31; Ephesians 2:2). Passages like 2 Corinthians 2:6-8 show us that such spirit powers are real, that they were involved in bringing about the death of Christ (albeit by human agents – cf John 13:27) in the hope that this would thwart the purposes of God, and that their end is assured. Moreover, such spirit powers are still at work, through a variety of agencies (cf Ephesians 6:10-20; Colossians 2:13-15).

The New Testament, however, adds an important element to our understanding. It tells us that in Christ and his death such forces have been beaten once and for all (Colossians 3:15). In the cross a cosmic battle was conducted during which the forces of evil were disarmed, publicly exposed, and led in triumphal procession (cf Hebrews 2:14; 1 John 3:8).

The only real protection from such powers is therefore found in Jesus alone. While demonic powers still attempt to drag us away from Christ and to deceive us in our thinking, the message of the cross is that Satan has been defeated and that we need to draw on the resources offered to us in our union with him. We need to appropriate the good news of Jesus and apply it in our day to day living and our very real continuing spiritual conflict with the forces of darkness (Ephesians 6:10-20).

This whole area of angels, spirit powers, and spiritual warfare is much discussed in Christian circles these days and parallels a vast upsurge in interest in the occult and New Age religion outside Christian circles. There is also increasing literature available, much of which owes more to the speculative minds of its writers than to biblical thought. A good introductory and balanced book to what the Bible has to say on these things, which also gives some realistic and practical advice on how it applies today, is *Powers of Darkness*, by Clinton E. Arnold (Leicester, Inter-Varsity Press, 1992).

(d) The Revelation Continued

While the messenger continued to speak Daniel again *bowed with his face toward the ground and was speechless,* whereupon *the one who looked like a man touched* his lips and Daniel opened his *mouth and began to speak.* What he had firstly expressed in actions, he in turn expressed in words: *'I am overcome with anguish because of the vision, my lord. My strength is gone and I can hardly breathe.'*

For the third time *the one who looked like a man touched* Daniel and *gave* him *strength.* Having been encouraged, Daniel felt fortified to hear what the man had to say. The messenger said:

> *'Do you know why I have come to you? Soon I will return to fight against the prince of Persia, and when I go, the prince of Greece will come; but first I will tell you what is written in the Book of Truth. (No one supports me against them except Michael, your prince. And in the first year of Darius the Mede, I took my stand to support and protect him.)'*

In previous dreams, visions, and revelations, Daniel had come to understand that there were two nations in view which will have authority over God's people and will therefore pose significant threat to them, or at least to God's purposes for them. The two nations were Persia and Greece. The messenger facing Daniel was God's messenger. He represented God and his purposes and therefore supported the people of God and opposed the nations of Greece and Persia and their princes. Daniel was for God and therefore for the people of God and so he found support in *Michael,* the *prince* of Israel. This alliance had already been seen *in the first year of Darius the Mede* when God's messenger took his *stand to support and protect* Michael (possibly a reference to the fall of Babylon under Cyrus which also posed significant threat for the people of God).

Earlier in the chapter we were told that the messenger left the conflict in the hands of Michael in order to bring a message to Daniel in response to his seeking God. In verses 20-21 the messenger told Daniel he would *return to fight against* the imminent danger posed by *the prince of Persia* and *the prince of Greece* but first he would tell him what was *written in the Book of Truth.* The *Book of Truth* referred to a book whose content detailed the future purposes of God in his world (cf the scroll of Revelation 5). It would be this purpose that the nations (and the powers which lay behind them) threatened to thwart.

3. If God Is For Us . . .

The picture in this chapter is a grand one. On an individual level God is eager to hear the prayers of his saints, eager to encourage and strengthen them, and eager to inform them of his purposes for his people. His people are of great importance to him.

On a national level, he is also for his people. His purposes for his people are being fought out not only on earth but in heaven. He continually seeks their best interests and provides what is needed to accomplish these interests.

On a cosmic level, he is God. Although the nations and their spiritual representatives seem to pose a threat to him and his purposes and although it seems at times that they have been victorious (cf Daniel 8:9-12), there is a Book of Truth or a scroll of destiny which reveals that God is the Lord of history, who orders history and brings it to its conclusion. This God is sovereign and almighty. There is no ultimate threat to him, to his purposes, or to his people.

In Romans 5:1-5 Paul tells us that if we are Christians we have been justified through faith, we have peace with God, and we therefore rejoice in hope of the glory of God. This hope will never disappoint us because 'God has poured out his love into our hearts by the Holy Spirit, whom he has given to us.' The Holy Spirit reminds us of all that God has done for us in Christ and in his cross and thereby assures us that we are right with God. Because of the cross we know that God is for us.

In Romans chapter 8 Paul develops this further. Recalling the language of justification used in chapter 5 he goes on to say that it is this justification by Christ that assures us of God's fatherly goodwill towards us (Romans 8:28-39). Our representative in heaven is not a nameless messenger, as in Daniel 10, but God's own Son who has taken on the forces of darkness and defeated them. This Son has demonstrated beyond a shadow of doubt that God is for his people whom he foreknew. He has battled the great adversary and won. Nothing that happens to the people of God is outside his sphere of activity and no force in the world, physical or spiritual, can separate them from his love and his purposes of redemption and life. Our future is secured. If God is for us, who can be against us?

FOR STUDY, DISCUSSION AND PRAYER

1. What is the significance of the setting of Daniel 10-12?

2. In the Old Testament God is said to be 'a man of war' (cf Exodus 15:3ff; Deuteronomy 33:1-2; Judges 5:19-20; 2 Samuel 5:22-24). Do you think this concept carries through to the New Testament and to us today? How?

3. Read Ephesians 6:10-20. How do we 'put on the full armour of God'? What does each of the elements of armour mean?

4. How do we know that God is 'for us'? What practical implications does this have for us as Christians?

24

Bright Shining As The Stars 11:1-12:13

1. The Contents Of The Book Of Truth

Chapter 11 of Daniel poses significant problems for the reader of Daniel. On the one side, the book has led us to think of Daniel as a man of the sixth century BC serving at the courts of various Babylonian and Persian kings. On the other side, chapter 11 provides us with a mine of detailed information regarding the Persian and Greek periods, with a focus on the reigns of Antiochus III and Antiochus IV Epiphanes. This leads us to think that a second century person might be responsible.

As noted in chapter 2, the position taken in this commentary is that the sixth century historical person of Daniel is the source of not only the stories, but also the visions. Daniel *did* dream about the future of his people, and about events that would happen in the future, and he did record these dreams for those who would follow.

At the same time, the relevance of his dreams for the second century and the detail reflected in this chapter may mean the final writing up of his life and dreams might not have taken place until a time when people saw some of the things he dreamt about happening before their very eyes.

After emphasising the dependability of the revelation, the messenger of chapter 10 begins his recounting of what is written in the Book of Truth (10:21).

(a) Persia

Cyrus, the current monarch, is the first Persian king. The messenger foretold that there will be *three more kings* after him (cf Daniel 7:6). Rather than taking the phrase literally, it may be better to understand the phrase 'three . . . and a fourth' in the way it is used in Proverbs 30 and Amos 1-2, that is, to emphasise the final element of the sequence. Such a metaphorical usage finds support in the second half of the sentence where we are told of the fourth king, *who will be far richer than all the others.* His wealth will lead to *power*, which will in turn lead to confrontation with *the kingdom of Greece.*

(b) Alexander the Great

From the Book of Truth it was recounted that *a mighty king will appear* (that is, Alexander the Great). This king it was said, *will rule with great power and do as he pleases.* However, this king's appearance will be short-lived. *His empire will be broken up and parcelled out toward the four winds of heaven* (that is, split asunder and fragmented) rather than the normal process in which it would *go to his descendants.* Because of its fragmentation, those who received the kingdom would not *have the power* which Alexander had enjoyed.

(c) Kings Of The North And South

Out of the division of the kingdom, it was said, two kings and kingdoms will emerge which will have special import for the people of God There will be the king of the South (that is, Egypt, headed by the Ptolemaic dynasty) and the king of the North (that is, Syria and Babylonia, headed by the Seleucid dynasty and begun by Seleucus I, referred to as, the commander who *will rule his own kingdom*, 11:5). These two kingdoms will war against each other, attempt alliances, and act treacherously with each other. As had often happened before, with power blocs in the North and South of the fertile crescent, Palestine would find itself caught in the middle and often a battleground for opposing forces. As a result Jews would inevitably take sides and seek opportunities (verse 14), sometimes with religious motivation (that is, *'in fulfilment of the vision'*. This is perhaps, a reference to the vision of Daniel 8). On this occasion they would not meet with success.

The northern king (a reference to Antiochus III), however, would meet with success, gaining firm control of Palestine, Phoenicia, and even Judea (*'the Beautiful Land'*, verse 16). Rather than push on to make his defeat of the South complete through warfare, the messenger stated that, he will enter into another alliance by marriage (verse 17), betrothing his daughter to the king of the South (Ptolemy V). The ploy will *not succeed or help him* and so he will turn *his attention to the coastlands* and take *many of them*. Like many before him, buoyed on by success he will overreach himself and in his *insolence* take on *a commander* greater than himself (that is, Rome) who will *put an end to his insolence and turn his insolence back upon him*. The messenger continued asserting that with his son (Antiochus IV) hostage in Rome Antiochus will return to Syria only to *stumble and fall* (that is, be assassinated). Again, like many before him, after greatness he will be *seen no more*.

The successor of this king of the North (Seleucus IV) would be faced with having to pay the tribute caused by his father's overreaching of himself. To do so he would *send out a tax collector. In a few years, however, he will be destroyed, yet not in anger or in battle* (he may have been assassinated) and *will be succeeded by a contemptible person who has not been given the honour of royalty* (that is, Seleucus's younger brother Antiochus IV).

(d) A Contemptible Person

According to the messenger this contemptible person will seize power *through intrigue*, sweep away opposition, depose the current Jewish High Priest and murder him (*a prince of the covenant will be destroyed*), seizing rich lands and acquiring wealth. He will make two campaigns against the king of Egypt and plot to destroy his nephew in the South (11:25-30a).

He will also resolve to destroy all those in Palestine who are loyal to the covenant God made with his people, setting his heart *against the holy covenant*. His second invasion South will not be as successful as intended. As had happened with his father, he will be reduced to size and forced to bow to the superior might of *the western coastlands* (that is, a reference to 'Kittim' – cf Numbers 24:24. Here Rome is probably meant). History tells us that in this absence, perhaps with support of conservative Jews, there was a change of High Priest, with the new incumbent anti-Syrian and therefore pro-Egyptian. As a result, this contemptible person will *vent his fury against the holy covenant. He will return to his land and show favour to those who forsake the holy covenant.* To this end, he will stop at the Holy City, Jerusalem, on his way back from Egypt and enter the temple and plunder its sacred treasures (11:25-28). He will then act to *abolish the daily sacrifice.* With the force of *his armed forces* he will *set up the abomination that causes desolation.* In all of this he will be aware that only the faithful people of God will resist. They (that is, the *hasidim* or 'committed' of 1 Maccabees 2:42) act as expected, resisting even under brutal persecution, pillaging, death and imprisonment. Nevertheless persecution continues (11:29-35). Unlike the faithful of Daniel 1-6 they will not receive miraculous divine intervention. True, some *will receive a little help* (perhaps the encouragement of the first Judean guerillas and activists – cf 1 Maccabees 2-4) and as a result *many who are not sincere* (that is, shallow in their commitment to the cause) *will join them*. However, *some of the wise will stumble*. Such persecution and testing will be the means of accomplishing refining and purifying.

It is at this point in the revelation that the picture painted becomes quite blurred and unclear. The messenger's story moves more and more into the future, lapsing more and more into the language of chapters 7 and 8. Antiochus never quite disappears from the scene or the focus of the revelation, but he increasingly becomes a pattern for the many who would follow him. Like those who have gone before him (cf Isaiah 14) he will *exalt and magnify himself above every god and will say unheard-of things against the God of gods*.

Finally his end will become a pattern for the end of those who would follow him. Like all those who step out from under the king of heaven's rule this king will succeed, but only until God chooses to put an end to it (11:36-39).

With verses 40-45 the telescopic lens focuses even more on the distant future, stating that there will be opposition and the falling of many nations. The language bears more and more reminiscences of Old Testament prophecies against the enemies of God and portrayals of their ultimate demise. There will be an affront against the people of God and the land of God's people (*'he will invade the Beautiful Land'*). His kingdom and power will be extended. As Sennacherib heard rumours as he defied God outside Jerusalem (Isaiah 36-37; cf 2 Kings 19), so rumours will alarm this one who defies God. They will cause him to retreat and spark him into a final great rage in which he destroys and annihilates many. Finally he will pitch his tents in the land of the one he has set himself against, the King of heaven, and as the prophets predicted this enemy of God will at last be destroyed. This profaner of

God will meet his end at the gates of the city of the God he had defied. *He will come to his end, and no one will help him.*

Antiochus is representative of a type. He is one of many who had come before him, have since come after him, and will continue to come until the end of the world. Daniel 11:40-45 is saying that he will come to an end as the result of God's activity. Because he is like so many before him many of the circumstances of his end will be like those who had preceded him. Verses 11:40-55 are not meant to be literal, but pictorial.

(e) The Time of Distress

At the announcement of the end of Antiochus, it is as if the camera pans back behind the scenes and focuses on heaven again where *Michael, the great prince* will be active. The distress that will come upon the earth will be enormous, *such as has not happened from the beginning of nations until then.* There will be many deaths, the godly and ungodly alike will die. Together *they will sleep in the dust of the earth* and together they will awake from sleep to judgment. *Multitudes will awake, some to everlasting life, others to shame and everlasting contempt. Those who are wise,* that is, those *whose name is found written in the book of life,* who have been faithful to the God of heaven like the wise man Daniel, who have led *many to righteousness* through their faithfulness, will *shine like the brightness of the heavens.* Their glory will be *like the stars for ever and ever.*

(f) A Resurrection Of The Dead

Daniel 12:2 is the most developed statement regarding resurrection in the Old Testament. Daniel is emphatic. Death cannot be the end. God will not permit life to end with the grave and will therefore raise the dead (even though the raising of the dead referred to here is probably not the raising of all the dead, but the raising of Israelite dead). The ones who live in reliance upon him will rise to everlasting life while the ones who have denied him and continued to live in independence will rise to everlasting shame.

Even in Daniel 12, the picture is therefore incomplete. The resurrection is related to this specific conflict and this specific situation. It is far from universal.

Between the Testaments there was much further development and the rise of a number of different positions regarding the after-life (cf the Pharisees and Saducees of the New Testament, see Acts 23:8). With the coming of Jesus the Bible's doctrine of resurrection reaches full flower. For the first time resurrection becomes more than a hope. It becomes a certainty. Jesus rose from the dead and as he rose so shall we. He was the first fruit of those who are asleep (1 Corinthians 15:20). Moreover, all shall be raised: some to life, and some to everlasting contempt (John 5:24-30).

2. The End Of The Revelation

The messenger's account ended at this point and he urged Daniel to close up and *seal the words* of the scroll and to keep them safe *until the time* when they would be needed.

Then, as Daniel stood there beside the river Tigris where the vision had first come to him, he saw two other figures, one on each *bank of the river*, engaging in conversation with Daniel's messenger. One asked *the man clothed with linen, 'How long will it be before these astonishing things are fulfilled?'*

In response the man raised his hands toward heaven in solemn oath and Daniel *heard him swear by him who lives forever, saying, 'It will be for a time, times, and half a time. When the power of the holy people has been finally broken, all these things will be completed.'* The point of their conversation is that there will be a time and a place when persecution.will reach its absolute maximum. A time when the people of God will endure their greatest agony as they are tortured, unjustly tried and foully treated. At this time God will act, delivering and rescuing just as he did with Daniel, Shadrach, Meshach and Abednego (12:4-7).

Although Daniel *heard*, he *did not understand* and expressed his lack of understanding to the messenger who replied to him:

> '*Go your way, Daniel, because the words are closed up and sealed until the time of the end. Many will be purified, made spotless and refined, but the wicked will continue to be wicked. None of the wicked will understand, but those who are wise will understand.*
>
> *From the time that the daily sacrifice is abolished and the abomination that causes desolation is set up, there will be 1,290 days. Blessed is the one who waits for and reaches the end of the 1,335 days.*'

Daniel did not understand what this meant. He wondered what the final outcome would be. He was to be disappointed. It was not revealed to him. What was revealed was that wickedness will continue to be part of the world in which he lived, suffering would continue to be used by God as part of the purifying process through which his people pass (cf Daniel 11:33-35). The wise who fear God would continue to understand this (12:8-10).

The answer came to the question on the mind of every wise person, 'How long?' Yet the answer was an obscure one. Again, although the numbers can be figured in such a way as to fit various events at the time of Antiochus, it is the general point that is of significance. It appears to be that persecution will occur and will at the time seem unlimited. However, it is limited, and knowing this the wise person should endure for that extra period. At the right time, the decreed time, God will come, deliver, vindicate and end history (12:11-13).

3. Daniel And The Events Of The Second Century

On return from his first campaign in Egypt, Antiochus entered and plundered the temple. On return from his second campaign he took further repressive actions and official persecution began. Proclamations were issued directing Jews to adopt foreign customs, banning burnt offerings and sacrifices, prohibiting circumcision and profaning the Sabbath and Jewish feasts. Similarly altars and shrines were built for idols where pigs and other unclean animals were sacrificed. Those who would not comply or join in were put to death. Eventually the 'abomination of desolation' was erected in the Temple.

For many, this was the last straw. They could go no further and decided that they would lay down their lives rather than give up their faith. When the inspectors appointed by Antiochus arrived in villages and towns directing the inhabitants to offer sacrifice one after the other to pagan gods, they refused. Because of their resistance a number were tortured and died at the hands of the troops.

In one incident Antiochus sent Apollonius at the head of an army of twenty-two thousand men to Jerusalem. Upon arrival he pretended that he had come in peace only to order his men to parade fully armed on the Sabbath day and then slaughter all those who came out to watch.

On another occasion, two women were charged with not having kept the law by circumcising their children. The troops killed the children. They hung them at the breasts of the women, parading them publicly around the town and then hurled them over the city wall.

Later seven brothers were arrested with their mother. The king tried to force them to taste pig's flesh by torturing them with whips and scourges. When they refused the king's anger rose and he brutally tortured them one by one.

It was against this background that many pondered the question Daniel pondered: 'How is it that God allows such things to happen? Where is God when such things happen? If God really is in control, then when will he cause such things to cease? When will he act to end such evil and suffering?'

To Jews of the second century and to others facing similar situations and asking similar questions, the last three chapters of the book of Daniel speak poignantly. In dark hours such chapters bring hope to God's people, because they bring God to them. He proves to be a God who was not distant, removed or uninvolved, but who is active in history, and whose kingdom is assured.

4. Life and Death

These chapters of Daniel also capture a great reality of Scripture and of Christian experience. As Christians we believe in a God who is not only great and sovereign, but is also good. The Bible and experience teach us that evil has entered the world and is maintained in the world by demonic and human agents. Such agents set themselves against this good and great God and seek to overthrow him and his purposes. They also set themselves against all those who would line themselves up with this good and great God. Therefore, violent opposition and perhaps even violent death awaits those who desire God and seek his purposes.

One of the uncanny things about the message of the Bible and indeed of the gospel is, it is that very opposition that so often becomes the means by which God's purposes are achieved. It is at the cross that principalities and powers are defeated. It is in weakness and persecution that God's strength is made manifest. It is in the foolish message of the cross that God's wisdom becomes plain. God's pattern is that life comes through death. Paul captured it brilliantly in 2 Corinthians 4:7-12 and 16-18.

> But we have this treasure in jars of clay to show that this all-surpassing power is from God and not from us. We are hard pressed on every side, but not crushed; perplexed, but not in despair; persecuted, but not abandoned; struck down, but not destroyed. We always carry around in our body the death of Jesus, so that the life of Jesus may also be revealed in our body. For we who are alive are always being given over to death for Jesus' sake, so that his life may be revealed in our mortal body. So then, death is at work in us, but life is at work in you...

> Therefore we do not lose heart. Though outwardly we are wasting away, yet inwardly we are being renewed day by day For our light and momentary troubles are achieving for us an eternal glory that far outweighs them all. So we fix our eyes not on what is seen, but on what is unseen. For what is seen is temporary, but what is unseen is eternal.

FOR STUDY, DISCUSSION AND PRAYER

1. Read 1 Corinthians 15. Summarise Paul's main
    points regarding the doctrine of the resurrection in
    this passage.

2. List some of the main similarities and differences in
    the way Daniel talks about the fate of God's people in
    Daniel 1-6 and 7-12.

3. What does 2 Corinthians 4:7-18 tell us about the
    expectations we should have as Christians?

4. Use 2 Corinthians 4:7-18 as the basis of prayer for
    yourself and other Christians with whom you have
    relationships.

25

Understanding the Kingdom of God (IV)

As we have gone through the book we have discovered various strands of thinking about the kingdom of God. We have seen that the primary theme of the book of Daniel is the kingdom of God and that the various elements of his thinking on this topic tie together the book as a whole. Daniel is the first and only Old Testament book to deal with the kingdom of God in so frank and so full a way.

It is appropriate that we now put the whole picture together and summarise what we have found. As in earlier chapters, we can summarise using the following points:

- As the creator of the world, God is its one true King.

Throughout the book we are constantly hearing about the King of heaven, the God of gods, the King of kings. All that is in the world, stands under his kingly rule. He is the one who created the world and who controls its history. As the one who began the world he is the one who determines its course and its end.

- God's kingly rule of his world is characterised by justice and mercy.

The Bible's picture of God is that he is not a tyrant. Rather, he has the best interests of his world in mind. He is always merciful, always kind, always just, and always firm with those who resist his rule, whether they be his people or outsiders. In the book of Daniel we have seen this rule in action time and time again.

- God delegates his kingship to human beings.

Daniel picked up images from Genesis and Psalm 8 and showed that when God made human beings he made them in the image of God, exercising dominion under his overarching rule. Man is God's representative on earth, ruling the earth on God's behalf. Not only this, man is to copy the rule of God in his own rule. He is to rule the earth with justice and mercy, as God rules.

Because he is the King of kings and the giver of all rule and dominion and because he is sovereign, he gives his rule to whomever he wishes. The rule is his. He gives it and takes it as he pleases. He alone is King.

- Every human being must recognise that whatever rule he or she has is a gift from God, delegated by him.

Because man's rule is delegated rule, it is subject to a higher authority, the King of heaven. He is the Most High and all rule must act with him in mind. All human rule must 'raise its eyes towards heaven' (Daniel 4:34) and realise its derivative nature.

- Human beings can be divided into two groups: the wise and the foolish.

The wise are those who understand that there is a creator God who is king of all the earth. They know that reality is found with God and fear him. They live in this world with that understanding about reality undergirding everything they do and say.

The wise make practical, everyday choices about life based on their fear of God. Sometimes the choices they make are easy. Most of the time they are hard, because their fear of God and their allegiance to him throws them into opposition to a world which sees reality differently. Sometimes their choices are hard because they result in persecution and even death. However, the wise person knows that there is no alternative, God is where reality is found.

The foolish, on the other hand, are those who ignore the reality of God. They say in their hearts, 'There is no God' and they act as if this were so.

The foolish also make choices, but their decisions are based on the premise of God's absence or non-existence. In their choices they are therefore making themselves god, setting themselves against the God of heaven and therefore against his people.

• The kingly rule of God is both a promise and a threat.

God is the only real king of heaven. His kingly rule offers two alternative ends for the people of the earth.

On the one hand, those who are wise, recognising God's kingship and aligning themselves with him are offered a promise. The promise is that they will be on the victorious side. God will win and when he does he will vindicate his people, the wise ones, and they will rule his world on his behalf.

Sometimes these wise ones, the saints of the Most High, will experience God's victory in this present life, as Daniel, Shadrach, Meshach and Abednego did in Daniel 3 and 6. However, sometimes they will not experience it until after they die martyrs' deaths, as was the case for the wise ones of Daniel 7-12. No matter what, they will experience it. Their vindication is as certain as God's visible kingship over the earth. It is only a matter of time. Moreover, God will not leave them alone even when they suffer. In the midst of their suffering, the King of heaven will be with them.

On the other hand, the kingship of God offers a threat to the foolish. To all of those who will not fear God and who act as though there were no King of heaven or no God, the kingship of God comes with a threat of extinction. God will act against all the fools of this world, bringing them to an end. The models for such judgment in the book are Belshazzar and Antiochus Epiphanes.

Some fools will see apparent success and victory and give the appearance of having got away with scorning and ignoring God (for example, Antiochus – Daniel 7-12). However, in the end God will act to judge them and bring their reign to an end.

Other fools will not have to wait so long (for example, Belshazzar – Daniel 5). They will see God act very swiftly. He will not delay but will bring them to a speedy end.

- The kingship of God is headed toward a goal. It is the world living under God as King and the end of all rivals to his kingship.

Because God is creator and the only true King, there will be a time when all opposition to his kingship must cease. A day must come when the reality of heaven, Yahweh, the only King, will be reflected on earth. This will happen through the overthrow of earthly kingdoms and rulers and the establishment of God's kingdom. This is a sure, certain outcome of the kingship of God.

This kingdom of God will have as its leader *one like a Son of Man,* a Jewish human being who has lived under God's rule, a perfect man and perfect wise man. To one such as this God will give his authority, glory, and sovereign power. All peoples, nations and people of every language will worship him. His dominion will be an everlasting dominion. It will not pass away or ever be destroyed.

From a New Testament perspective we could add.

- Jesus is the only one who has exercised the rule of God perfectly. He is given the rule of God for all time.

Jesus was wise, living in the fear of God. He was perfect man, demonstrating man's dominion over the created order and ruling as God rules, with justice and mercy, always having the best interests of others in mind, laying down his life for their well-being. He lived under the rule of God, humbling himself and obeying God to the point of death, even death on a cross.

As a result God exalted him and gave him the name that is above every other name, that at the name of Jesus every knee should bow, in heaven and on earth and under the earth, and every tongue confess that Christ is Lord, to the glory of God the Father (Philippians 2:5-11).

Jesus is God's appointed ruler. The day will come when all creation will see him sitting at the right hand of the Most High and coming on the clouds of heaven to judge the world and to rule God's everlasting kingdom.

From Daniel we are able to conclude:

- He will in turn give the kingdom to the wise.

In Jesus, God will give the kingdom to the wise, that is to those who fear God (or in New Testament terms, to those who believe in Jesus). The heavenly Son of Man represents the saints of the Most High. He will receive the rule of God as one who has ruled as humans were ordained to rule. He will pass it on to those who live in fear of God. Only such people are fit to rule God's world. These are the poor in spirit and theirs is the kingdom of heaven.

26

Some Final Reflections

1. Daniel And Jesus

It is evident from the the New Testament that Jesus read the prophet extensively and became saturated with his thought and attitudes. For this reason, the teaching and thought of Jesus cannot be fully understood apart from the book of Daniel. Although we have seen this time and time again as we have read through Daniel and followed his thought through to the New Testament, it is helpful to summarise some of the significant connections.

(a) The Self Identity Of Jesus

Jesus lived in a world where there was a huge messianic expectation. Jews longed for deliverance and vindication. They had put up with Greek regimes and now they were suffering under Roman tyrants. They longed for a victorious Messiah of the type outlined in Psalm 2, that is, one who would challenge the nation of Rome and lead the nation of Israel in victorious revolt against this pagan nation.

Jesus chose to reject such political expectations. In their place he chose to identify himself as the heavenly human 'son of Man'. Such a Son of Man, like the saints of the Most High and the servant of Isaiah, would come into rule and authority only through humility, suffering, rejection and seeming defeat. His rule would not be dynamic and politically forceful, but surprising, eternal and obviously the gift of God.

(b) Jesus and the Kingdom

Jesus used Daniel's language. He did not talk about the rule of God, like the prophets before Daniel had done. He talksed about the 'kingdom' of God (cf. Daniel 4:3, 34; 6:26) as Daniel had done.

Jesus also thought like Daniel. Daniel looked forward to a future day when God would act to bring in a new age and restore his people. So did Jesus. Daniel looked to a time when the saints would rule over God's world under God's overarching rule and so did Jesus (as did Paul after him – 1 Corinthians 6:2). There would be a time, as promised by Daniel, when the kingdom would come in power (cf. Mark 9:1).

Like Daniel, Jesus spoke of opposition to the rule of God, of pagan rulers who would set themselves up against God and his people. He told of nation rising against nation, of betrayals and floggings, of witnessing before kings and governors. He warned of the need to stand firm to the end, despite 'the abomination that causes desolation', and of the shortening of these days for the sake of the elect. Although he, like Daniel, did not know the time of the end, he knew its signs and led his disciples to wait expectantly for the time when 'men will see the Son of Man coming in the clouds with great power and glory' (cf Mark 13).

(c) Jesus and the Experiences of Daniel

Although we cannot tell from his words themselves, it appears that the man Daniel and his experiences in the face of conflict and opposition were formative in the life and ministry of Jesus.

Jesus accepted the way of life of the godly man as exemplified throughout the Scriptures. According to such passages as Psalm 22 and Psalm 69 the godly ought to expect rejection and persecution because of their trust in God. When this happens they must continue to trust God. Eventually God will act to deliver and vindicate them. This pattern is seen time and time again in the book of Daniel (for example, the fiery furnace, the lion's den, the persecution of the saints of the Most High).

Jesus was aware of the destiny that awaited the godly and perhaps as he headed towards Jerusalem and towards suffering (Luke 9:51) he found courage in the lives of Daniel and the other saints in his book. Perhaps it was the stories of Daniel, Shadrach, Meshach, Abednego and the saints of the Most High that convinced him that resurrection and vindication must occur as the aftermath of persecution (Luke 9:21-22).

In Jesus the clear message of Daniel resounded that victory comes through defeat, vindication through suffering, life through death. The path to life runs through the cross.

2. Daniel and John

The book of Daniel was a significant influence on the book of Revelation. In proportion to its length it contributes a far greater number of allusions than any other Old Testament book. So also it contributed to Revelation in thought, structure and theology.

Apart from allusions, the book of Revelation has four significant themes running through it which parallel those we have seen in the book of Daniel.

Believers live under hostile (beastly and tyrannical) world rulers and in the midst of a pagan society which continually pushes them towards compromise. If they do not compromise then persecution awaits them (Revelation 2; 11:1-13; 12:10-17; 13:5-18). Although they suffer under such persecution, they are ultimately victorious (Revelation 1:9, 18; 2; 5:5-9; 11:1-13; 12:11-17; 20:4-10). God progressively, often imperceptibly, pushes his kingdom on, finally wrapping up history and establishing his kingdom (Revelation 1:6, 9; 2:7, 10, 13, 16, 26-27; 3:11, 21; 5:10; 20:4-6). At this time the saints experience final deliverance and vindication through the Lamb and based on his victory in the cross.

In Daniel we are let into heaven and shown that the conflict experienced by God's people with earthly kings is an expression of a greater heavenly or spiritual war being waged by God and his angels against heavenly, anti-God forces. So too with the book of Revelation, where heavenly battle and conflict involving angelic representatives is parallelled in the earthly experiences of persecution, deliverance and vindication.

3. Daniel and Us

I hope that this commentary has helped put the whole book of Daniel in perspective and begun to apply it to our contemporary situation. Again, it is helpful to summarise some conclusions and implications of our reading:

- It is wrong to use Daniel as some chart of world history, adding up numbers, performing calculations and figuring dates.

What is presented in the book of Daniel is not a precise prediction of the future of the world, but a philosophy of life, a world view. This world view comes out in the stories of chapters 1-6, as well as in the dreams and visions of 7-12.

- Without the book of Daniel, our view of Jesus would be impoverished.

The book of Daniel helps us understand many of the things of the New Testament that otherwise might be puzzling. It helps us understand some of those difficult passages such as Mark 13 with their strange language and complicated thoughts. It also helps us interpret them and makes sense of them. Perhaps, having read Daniel, we are also better equipped to make an assault on reading the book of Revelation.

Having read Daniel we can now read the term 'Son of Man' in the New Testament with such passages as Daniel 2, 4, and 7 as well as Genesis 1:27-28 and Psalm 8 coming to mind. We can understand why Jesus used the term and what he meant when he did. What is more the future aspects of Jesus' teaching on the kingdom of God assume new meaning and significance.

The book of Daniel also helps us to understand the confidence Jesus had about his resurrection in such passages as Mark 8:31.

> He then began to teach them that the Son of Man must suffer many things and be rejected by the elders, chief priests and teachers of the law, and that he must be killed and after three days rise again.

Maybe the emphasis in this prediction is not so much on the phrase 'after three days,' but on the conviction Jesus had that he will rise again. Having read Daniel we can understand from where such conviction might have come. Daniel has clearly explained some consistently recurring patterns present in our world. On the one hand, our world lives in opposition to God and therefore persecutes the godly. On the other hand, there is also a pattern in the way God deals with those who are godly and persecuted for their faith. He will eventually rescue, deliver and vindicate. As Jesus was obviously well acquainted with the book of Daniel, he knew that God acted this way with Daniel, Shadrach, Meshach, Abednego and the wise of Daniel 12. He knew God would do the same with him. It is such Old Testament patterns that would have informed and reassured Jesus.

- God has not changed. The patterns seen in Daniel are patterns that always operate in God's dealings with the world and with his people.

We do not live in the ancient courts of Nebuchadnezzar and Belshazzar. Nor do most of us suffer under such rulers as Antiochus Epiphanes, Nero, Diocletian, or any of the other strongly anti-god rulers that succeeded them. Nevertheless, we do live in a world with negative attitudes toward God and toward those who choose to live for God. We do live in a world where the godly are persecuted because of their beliefs and practices. We are asked to do things that are ethically wrong, if not actually illegal. We face the consequences of our uncompromising stand for God and his values.

People in our world who have authority over us do not like us to have an allegiance that is prior to our allegiance to them. As a result there will be costs to pay, sometimes minor, but at other times major. The book of Daniel prepares us for such costs both by the example of Daniel and by the theology it conveys, and urges us to face them head on. Daniel tells us that such conflict must be entered into in the context of prayer and dependence upon God and promises us that he will not only be present with us, but also grant us the courage to withstand. He also tells us that while we can never be confident that we will always be rescued and vindicated in this life, final vindication and rescue from the greatest enemy, death, is inevitable and sure.

- Loyalty to God is greater than loyalty to people or even loyalty to country. Such loyalty demands willingness to sacrifice!

We all have loyalties, whether to families, relationships, bosses, or even ideas or philosophies. Daniel shows us that our loyalty to God must supplant all other loyalties. God must have first place.

Furthermore, Daniel demonstrates that a determination to serve God first inevitably leads to a willingness to serve him no matter what the cost in terms of security, money and health. Such fierce and sacrificial loyalty can be engaged in with cheerfulness and joy, for our God is the true God and life with him is life indeed.

- **The world is under judgment and therefore desperately in need of news of the Son of Man.**

The urgency of Daniel's visions and dreams can also spur us to evangelism. We know the truth that Christ has already come to die and through his death offer salvation. We also know that Jesus will come again as the heavenly Son of Man to judge the world for its rebellion against him. At this time only the saints of the Most High, that is, those who have lined themselves up with Jesus, will escape the pulverising judgment. In the light of Daniel's vision evangelism must be a priority for us. We must call people to turn away from their own kingdoms and enter into the kingdom of God's own Son.

- God is the King of heaven. He will dispose of all who abuse his rule and arrogantly flaunt the gift of rule he has bestowed on them.

Any evening television news bulletin these days will parade before us situations of war and desolation forced upon the world by tyrannical rulers. As we hear of people tortured and brutalised we too cry out with Daniel for an end to such inhuman behaviour.

Daniel tells us that we can find comfort. God has promised an end. A day will come when such rulers will be tossed aside by God and come to a swift and ignoble end because of their arrogance toward the King of heaven and their unwillingness to rule as he rules.

- The world was created good by God. It is to be lived in and enjoyed by his servants.

The book of Daniel is not otherworldly. It is spirited, down-to-earth and practical. Daniel lived in the world but was not of it. He lived in a pagan court and managed to not worry about trifling things, but about significant things. He saw his allegiance to God in perspective and made practical, everyday decisions about the exercise of that allegiance.

The book of Daniel encourages us to be equally determined and to examine our lives and challenges us where we are excessively scrupulous and start saying no where we are excessively liberal. We need to decide to retrain our consciences and weed out bits of unbiblical asceticism from our lives. Turning aside from asceticism we need to acknowledge with Paul that 'everything God created is good, and nothing is to be rejected if it is received with thanksgiving, because it is consecrated by the Word of God and prayer' (1 Timothy 4:4-5).

- Life in perspective, that is wise living, is life lived under the rule of God.

In Daniel we see a man in love with God and addicted to the Scriptures. Again and again we see him searching the Scriptures, consulting God, praying alone and praying in the company of God's people. Daniel knew that life under the rule of God was life under the Word of God. Time and time again he chose to live this way.

This is what it means to be truly human. It is to live in fellowship with God and in obedience to him. The big question of life, whether you were Daniel in Babylon, a Jew in the time of Antiochus Epiphanes, John in the first century, or a western Christian in the wealth and comfort of the twentieth century is, 'Am I living with God and for God?'

FOR STUDY, DISCUSSION AND PRAYER

1. Spend some time on your own jotting down the things you have learnt in your reading of Daniel concerning:

- God and his purposes.
- Yourself in relationship to God and his world and the people in it.
- The situations you face.

2. Write down areas in your life you think need to change as a result of what you have learnt.

3. Write down five specific changes you would like to implement in the next three months.

4. Share these things with a Christian friend, asking them to (1) pray with and for you for these changes to take place; and (2) check out how you are progressing with them on a regular basis.

Notes

Notes

Notes